Gianna Cassetta AND Ma

MW01256085

the caring teacher

Strategies for
Working Through
Our Own Difficulties
with Students

HEINEMANN
Portsmouth, NH

Heinemann

361 Hanover Street

Portsmouth, NH 03801–3912

www.heinemann.com

Offices and agents throughout the world

Library of Congress Cataloging-in-Publication Data
Names: Cassetta, Gianna, author. | Wilson, Margaret Berry, author.
Title: The caring teacher : strategies for working through our own
   difficulties with students / Gianna Cassetta, Margaret Wilson.
Description: Portsmouth, NH: Heinemann, 2019. | Includes bibliographical
   references. |
Identifiers: LCCN 2019016676 | ISBN 9780325088815
Subjects: LCSH: Teacher-student relationships. | Parent-teacher
   relationships. | Emotional intelligence. | Interpersonal communication.
   | Teacher effectiveness.
Classification: LCC LB1033 .C33 2019 | DDC 371.102/3—dc23
LC record available at https://lccn.loc.gov/2019016676

Acquisitions Editor: Margaret LaRaia
Production Editor: Patty Adams
Cover and Interior Design: Vita Lane
Typesetter: Gina Poirier Design
Manufacturing: Steve Bernier

Printed in the United States of America on acid-free paper

23 22 21 20 19 RWP 1 2 3 4 5

{ dedication }

From Gianna:

For Caleb and Sam, I love you more than love.

From Margaret:

To Andy and Matthew, with love.

table of contents

Acknowledgments   xi

Authors' Note   xv

introduction   How Much Should We Care
                   About Each Other?   1

**Considering How Relationships Impact
Children's Capacity to Learn**   2

Facing the Challenge of Caring for *Every* Child   5

Rethinking the Word *Normal*   6

Examining Our Biases   7

Changing Entrenched Negative Behaviors   8

Growing into Compassion   9

Recognizing Schools' Institutional Bias   10

Cultivating Our Willingness to Help   12

{**commitment**} Track Disciplinary Practices   15

section 01   Your Feelings Matter   17

{**difficulty**} Juan Felt Disliked   17

{**shift**} Recognize the Impact of Your Negative Feelings   19

→ {**strategy**} Evaluate Your Emotions   22

→ {**commitment**} Shift to Empathy   23

→ {**strategy**} Value Student and Family Feedback   27

→ {**commitment**} Take the Family's or Child's Point of View   28

→ {**strategy**} Invite a Trusted Colleague to Observe   29

→ {**strategy**} Videotape Yourself   30

→ {**strategy**} Keep Track of Your Interactions with Students   31

section 02   What Children Need   32

{**difficulty**} Willy Was Marked by Trauma   32

{**shift**} Focus on Assets, Not Deficits   36

→ {**strategy**} Assess Children's Self-Perceived Agency   42

→ {**strategy**} Value Approximation   44

→ {**commitment**} Examine Asset and Deficit Labeling   47

section 03   Language That Builds Relationships   49

{**difficulty**} Carlos Had a Bad Reputation   49

{**shift**} Change Your Internal Dialogue   52

→ {**strategy**} Switch to Growth-Oriented Language   53

→ {**commitment**} Plan Asset-Based Language   56

→ {**strategy**} Develop Compassionate Curiosity   57

→ {**commitment**} Reframe Your Thinking   58

→ {**strategy**} Change Your Mind-Set Through Positive Actions   59

→ {**commitment**} Brainstorm Positive Actions   60

→ {**strategy**} Practice Mindful Attention   61

→ {**strategy**} Attend to Your Life Beyond School   62

{**shift**} Change Your Public Conversations   63

  → {**strategy**} Talk More to Explore Solutions   65

  → {**strategy**} Use a Conversation Protocol   67

{**shift**} Change How You Speak to Children   75

  → {**strategy**} Use a Genuine Tone   77

  → {**strategy**} Address Actions, Not Character   78

   → {**commitment**} Replace Problematic Language   81

  → {**strategy**} Speak Directly and Privately to Students   82

  → {**strategy**} Match Language to Intent   83

   → {**commitment**} Use Intentional Language   86

section 04   Relatedness   87

{**difficulty**} Charlotte Felt Out of Sync   87

{**shift**} Intentionally and Continuously Foster Class Community   89

  → {**strategy**} Build Community Right from the Start   90

  → {**strategy**} Teach Community Expectations   96

  → {**strategy**} Use Class Rules as an Anchor All Year   98

  → {**strategy**} Engage in Daily Community Meetings   100

  → {**strategy**} Foster Inclusion and Compassion   103

  → {**strategy**} Use Challenging Social Situations
as Teachable Moments   104

  → {**strategy**} Pair and Group Students in Varied Ways   105

  → {**strategy**} Notice When Students Are Absent   106

  → {**strategy**} Find Ways to Connect Individually   107

→ {**strategy**} Cultivate Appreciation and Care   108

 → {**commitment**} Learn More About Individual Students   110

→ {**strategy**} Incorporate Shared and Meaningful
                  Academic Experiences   112

  → {**commitment**} Find Opportunities for Relatedness
                     in Your Curriculum   113

→ {**strategy**} Connect Social and Academic Learning   114

 → {**commitment**} Teach the Social Skills Your Students Need   117

<table>
<tr><td>section</td></tr>
<tr><td>**05**</td></tr>
</table>

Competence   118

{**difficulty**} Ricardo Gave Up Before Trying   118

{**shift**} Provide Multiple Opportunities to Develop Competence   121

 → {**commitment**} Assess a Child's Strengths   127

→ {**strategy**} Use Language That Fosters Competence   128

 → {**commitment**} Rehearse Language That Promotes
                    Competence   133

→ {**strategy**} Teach Students to Reflect and Self-Assess   135

 → {**commitment**} Plan Opportunities for Students
                    to Self-Assess   139

section
06 Autonomy   140

{**difficulty**} Alfred Was Seeking Control   140

{**shift**} Intentionally Cultivate Students' Autonomy   142

➤ {**strategy**} Gradually Share Responsibility   143

➤ {**commitment**} Shift Ownership to Students   144

➤ {**strategy**} Involve Students in Class Decision-Making   145

➤ {**strategy**} Offer Choice   153

➤ {**commitment**} Identify and Expand on Social and Academic Choices   156

➤ {**strategy**} Foster Autonomy Through Curriculum   157

{**shift**} Collaborate with Students   158

➤ {**strategy**} Use a Protocol for Teacher-Student Conversations   159

conclusion
Looking Inward and Outward   171

Works Cited   173

acknowledgments

From Gianna:

I first started thinking about writing this book because of my son Caleb. Caleb is a natural athlete. One of my favorite memories of him is watching him as a shaggy-haired three-year-old dribbling a soccer ball all the way around the reservoir in New York City's Central Park. At fifteen, he is a graceful, composed, and respected leader on the soccer field. On the pitch, Caleb looks and feels most connected to others, is technically skillful, and is able to make creative decisions that lead to scoring. Even when things get hard for him and he is not at his best, in soccer, he has strategies to work through it. Most of his experiences in the classroom, however, have not been quite as positive as his experiences on the field. In the classroom, he does not feel relatedness, competence, or autonomy.

Everyone has strengths and challenges, and all have places where they truly shine. I've known dozens and dozens of Calebs. I knew how exceptional they were outside of traditional academics if I put enough effort into knowing my students, and that helped me build a bridge for them in the classroom. I also know that too often, we don't put that effort into knowing our students. And deep down, I know that if Caleb weren't protected by his all-American looks, his educated parents, and his privilege, his school experience would have been far more damaging.

A family member once asked, "What are you going to do about it?"—meaning, how was I going to get him to be as successful in school as in soccer? Often, the questions we choose to ask reveal not only what we wonder but what we value. Consider the difference between the question "What are you going to do about it?" and the questions "How do you feel about Caleb's strengths and struggles?" "What are you doing to make sure Caleb is successful enough in school that he can really focus on his passion for soccer?" and "Since Caleb doesn't love academics, how will you cultivate the strengths he does have?"

Our culture tells us to view Caleb in a deficit model despite his strengths. Our culture sometimes tells us to ignore his strengths because academic performance is what matters; it's what will get you ahead in this world; it's the way to get a piece of the pie. And hence the question was "What are you going to do about it?"

If Caleb, a child of such privilege, can be viewed in a deficit model, what does that say for children who have no such protection? That made the answer to the question ("What are you going to do about it?") pretty clear. I'd begin writing this book.

Many people have taught me to be a more caring teacher, and I still continue to learn from and reflect on what I learned from them even years ago. Three people in particular have had an enormous impact on me. I met Terrance Kwame-Ross while still a school leader in New York City, and he helped me not only become more empathetic to the students I struggled to connect with but also think about social and emotional support at a systems level through a leadership lens. I met my coauthor close to ten years ago when starting a school in Denver. Margaret Berry Wilson became a trusted advisor and coach for me and many of my staff, and she pushed me, always in kind and practical ways, to rethink practices that had become habit but were not always the most compassionate ones for children. Brook Sawyer, who coauthored *No More Taking Away Recess* and *Classroom Management Matters* with me, gave me new tools with which I could view and speak about the world of social and emotional learning with her straightforward and practitioner-friendly research interpretation.

Of course, the students I have taught, and their families, have taught me more than anyone else in the world could about where I hit or missed the mark in being a caring teacher. There are too many to name, but to the students of PS 198 in Manhattan, Future Leaders Institute in Harlem, and SOAR in Denver: I'll hold you forever in my heart.

Thank you so much to the amazing Heinemann team for your support throughout this process: Margaret LaRaia, our editor, who learned along with us and helped us hold a vision. Also, Patty Adams in production; Vita Lane in design; Krysten Lebel, our editorial coordinator; and Kim Cahill in marketing: thank you.

No set of acknowledgments would be complete without one for Marc Waxman—my husband, best friend, chief learning partner, and copilot in most things in life including life in schools. Thank you for always fully sharing in the journey to become more caring teachers.

From Margaret:

I was fortunate to begin my teaching career under the guidance of two great school leaders (whom I probably didn't appreciate enough at the time). On my first day, Ed Costello, my mild-mannered, soft-spoken principal, shared two ideas that had a lasting impact on my teaching. First, he told all of us new teachers that we should never allow ourselves to think that a child didn't belong in our classrooms. He went on to discuss how we might, obviously, raise concerns about a student and how to address those. But he emphasized that if we began those discussions with a belief that the child didn't belong in our classrooms, we'd have already given up and would not succeed. That idea struck such a chord with me and guided my interactions with children from that day forward. Ed's second piece of advice was that we teach every day with the goal of making students want to return the next day. He threw out some simple ideas for doing that, such as stopping our read-aloud at some critical moment in the book or previewing a particularly interesting learning experience we had planned for the next day. But he also emphasized how important it was to make sure that students felt cared for and were engaged in what they were learning. I have tried to live out that principle in every teaching situation I have found myself in since, whether with children or adults.

Kathy Woods, the head of the division I was working in as I began my teaching career, also provided immediate inspiration and had a lasting impact on my teaching. The summer before I started teaching, she gave all of us Ruth Charney's book *Teaching Children to Care*, introducing me for the first time to many of the ideas in this book and strongly shaping how I would approach teaching in the years to come. Kathy also taught me the importance of patience. She used a simple but powerful metaphor that as we teach, we are planting seeds, and some of our work, or seeds, may take longer to sprout than others. She helped me see that I needed to persevere with students and their families even if it seemed like what I was trying wasn't working. Over the years, she was such a mentor to me both professionally and personally, and although she has now passed away, a day doesn't go by that I don't think of her or some piece of wisdom she shared.

Ed and Kathy, along with many other inspirational colleagues, especially Paula Denton, Babs Freeman-Loftis, and Lara Webb, helped me form a positive, student-centered vision of teaching and more importantly helped me understand that it was my job to care for children and help them care for each other and to see how that looked in action. For that, I am eternally grateful.

I also want to express my gratitude to Gianna for the role she has played in my growth as an educator and for inviting me to collaborate on this book. I met her when I was a consultant for a school she had cofounded. Over several years, I worked with her and her staff to implement many of the strategies we discuss in this book. That work deeply affected my understanding of the benefits and challenges of implementing social and emotional learning, and I personally gained so much from the challenging and rich conversations I had with her, her husband, Marc, and Reed Dyer. The idea for this book was Gianna's, and I am honored that she asked me to join in her efforts. As has been true of most of the work I've done with Gianna, it had incredibly challenging moments as well as great moments of joy. Thanks to her for being such a direct, collaborative, and inspiring partner in this writing.

I also want to thank all the students and families I was privileged to teach and work with through the years. Whenever I write about teaching, I am inspired by remembering them, amazed at what I learned from them, and humbled to think of the many ways I could have taught or connected with them more effectively.

Thanks as well to the many people at Heinemann who supported Gianna and me in this process: Margaret LaRaia, our editor, who helped us shape our understanding and vision for the book and put up with my frequent struggles to meet deadlines; Patty Adams in production; Vita Lane in design; Krysten Lebel, our editorial coordinator; Kim Cahill in marketing; Sarah Fournier, who has offered so much logistical support; and Karla Vigil, who gave us critical feedback during the drafting process.

Finally, I want to thank my husband, Andy, who, on this project, as with anything I undertake, offered unwavering support and backed that up with concrete actions that gave me time and space to write. And I am eternally grateful to my son, Matthew, who has taught me so much about how children learn and what they need at school and who cheerfully accepted the hours I ignored him while working on this book.

Because who we are matters in the classroom, we want to share some information about ourselves. To teach and to talk about teaching children requires that we understand who we are. Of course, there are always parts of ourselves that we're less conscious of than others, but part of being a teacher is continually learning about who you are so that you can remove obstacles between you and the children you teach. Although we've obviously devoted a good bit of time to thinking about this, we, like everyone, are still very much works in progress. We know that the way we treat our students can be rooted in how we've been socialized to think and how the systems we live in help perpetuate that thinking—about gender, race, socioeconomic status, social status, sexual preference, culture. And we know that thinking can be especially problematic when it comes to working with students who have historically been marginalized and underserved.

Even as we wrote about students, we had to pay attention to our own biases coming up. There were times when our narratives seemed to imply the students were at fault for various challenges. Even in trying to spark our readers' proclivity toward empathy for children in order to establish more positive relationships, we displayed our own deficit thinking. But we have to continually fight that thinking and stop putting the blame on children. We have to stop thinking about students from the lens of deficit and become aware of students' potential and our responsibility for cultivating that potential for each and every student we teach.

The joy of being a teacher is that it's a process of ongoing discovery and growth. That can make it exhausting, too, when we don't feel like we have the resources or support we need. No matter what is happening around us, we have a valuable resource inside of ourselves: the ability to make a lifelong commitment to self-study. This includes the sometimes painful steps needed to change, so that the beliefs and behaviors we bring to the classroom are no longer obstacles that keep us from connecting with our students. Those of us who are white, as Margaret and I are, have to continuously and consciously work to recognize and deconstruct our own bias and our role in maintaining our privilege and power as a white people, in order to minimize the harm we do to others and maximize a positive impact.

This work is ongoing and we must always be learners. Over the years, we have been influenced by significant work by researchers and practitioners on culturally responsive and sustaining teaching. We would be remiss not to point to that as important work for us and for you as you read this book. Reading the work of experts in the field is critical follow-up to reading this book. Here are the writers whose work we have read, who have influenced us, and whom we urge you to read:

- Gloria Ladson-Billings
- Geneva Gay
- Lisa Delpit
- Sonia Nieto
- Paulo Freire
- Sara Lawrence-Lightfoot
- Zaretta Hammond
- Pedro Noguera

We also acknowledge there are other experts in the field beyond those we have listed. All of these statements might make it sound like we're very self-aware. We're trying. However, self-awareness requires ongoing self-monitoring as well as listening to and learning from others—our students, their families, growing understandings about identity and society and changing contexts, and the amazing and diverse range of experts in the field. We're here to help you get started on this journey.

How Much Should We Care About Each Other?

> *Mistakes are a fact of life. It is the response to the error that counts.*
>
> **Nikki Giovanni**
>
> *Black Feelings, Black Talk, Black Judgement*

You may say to yourself, as have I and many teachers I've met, supervised, and coached over the years, "We're just human—we can't care for everyone." At first glance, this statement seems eminently reasonable. It is just human to like some children more than others, just as we like some adults more than others. Some adults we choose to spend the rest of our lives with, others we interact with as pleasant acquaintances, and others we avoid completely. We have the parents we love meeting with and others who make us want to call in sick to avoid. We have the colleagues we go to dinner with and the others we pretend we don't see when we pass them in the supermarket. It's absolutely normal.

Is it normal to feel less affection for the child who doesn't seem to like us? For the child who hurts others, either physically or through words? For the child who has habits or opinions we find distasteful? Yes, it's normal.

It's normal, but it has a hefty price for the child. The actions we don't take (not greeting a child warmly; not being eager to learn who she is, what she cares about and wants to know, and what information, experiences, and culture she brings into the classroom; and not figuring out how to help that child transcend difficulty) and the actions we do take because we feel it is our right (showing disdain for a child, using punishment to motivate a child, limiting a child's opportunity for engagement and agency in her learning) create a cage around that child, restraining her from exploring the world and becoming a fully realized human being in the classroom and the school community.

And our actions carry a price for us too. They limit us. They isolate us from the children and families we could be connected to, and when the actions become part of our daily interactions with others, they define us as angry, frightened, overwhelmed, and uncertain.

As professionals who have chosen to work with children, we must ask ourselves these questions: How can we be OK with liking many of our students so much less than others? How can we be OK with feeling defeated by them, feeling challenged or threatened, or ignoring them?

These can be uncomfortable questions. But the uncomfortable questions are often the most salient ones to ask ourselves. If we choose to self-monitor, to be metacognitive, to really listen to our thoughts and feelings, we can allow the discomfort to tell us we have some important work to do.

The reality is that something's not working in schools; many of us would say a lot isn't working. Educators, teachers especially, aren't held in particularly high esteem in our country, and the salaries, evaluation practices, and public comments are evidence of that. It's easy to follow the momentum of that negativity, which often leaves us feeling like victims of a system rather than agents of change. But if we look at the data—whether it is teacher turnover data, student suspension data, or school-to-prison pipeline data—we know that redefining ourselves as agents of change is the only way we are going to fix things.

This book's intention is to create space and a pathway for you to find your way to that agency, which will result in caring relationships between you and your students.

Considering How Relationships Impact Children's Capacity to Learn

One of Margaret's experiences as a coach illuminates the negative downward spiral that comes from not reckoning with our feelings. Once she was observing a third-grade teacher in action. All year she had heard from Derek about how challenging his class was and how one student in particular, Allen, was awful—disrespectful, impossible, and unmotivated. So Margaret went to watch. The lesson was a disaster. No sooner had Derek started to speak than Allen interrupted him to ask, "Why are we doing this? This is pointless."

Derek looked at him with disgust and maybe a little fear, apparently realizing that little he did or said would change the child's behavior, and said, "Stop interrupting." In that moment, Allen stopped, but he made his feelings known in other ways—through loud sighs, eye rolls, and under-the-breath comments. But then he interrupted again a few minutes later with another sarcastic comment. And so it continued. Derek was able to get the directions out in fits and starts, and most students finally started on their assignment, but Allen never did. Instead he sat slouched in a posture universally recognized as meaning, "You can't make me do this," and responded with increasing defiance to the teacher's threats of what was going to happen if he didn't get to work. From this observation, several things were apparent: (1) Derek appeared to be right that this child demonstrated behaviors that are often described as problematic in the classroom setting, (2) Derek did not like the child, and (3) the child absolutely knew it.

And then, serendipitously, the next day Margaret had the chance to see the same child and class with a different teacher, Shelly, who was doing a demonstration lesson. Shelly had taught many of the students, including Allen, the year before. She had built strong relationships with them, and it was evident from the moment she sat in front of them that she cared for them—Allen in particular. Her feelings were as obvious as those of the teacher the day before—she smiled warmly, greeted them, hugged Allen and a few others, and then told them she had picked out a book especially for them. She said she knew they would love it, and she winked at Allen as if to say, "I thought of you especially when I picked it out." And for an hour, that class, including Allen, looked like different students from the ones the day before. They were engaged, cooperative, and smiling, even though, as Shelly would later admit she regretted, she kept them sitting on the carpet with her for an hour, far longer than was appropriate for third graders.

We have had too much experience in the real world to think that one teacher's ability to care for Allen explained all the difference between these two classrooms or that learning to like a student is some type of magic cure for all of that student's troubles. Obviously, there was more at play here than how Shelly felt about her students. Her lesson was strong and addressed bullying, a topic Allen and his classmates were all concerned about, in a really interesting way. She had indeed chosen a great book. Her lesson was engaging and interactive as well.

We are not throwing stones at Derek; Allen's behaviors could be challenging. Even Shelly, who cared for him a great deal, knew this. Learning was not easy for him, and so planning lessons that included him and created an adjusted pathway on which he could be successful took time and effort. He required frequent check-ins to stay connected emotionally and checks for understanding to stay connected intellectually. His teacher had to consider which seating locations, resources, and support structures Allen needed on a daily, if not hourly, basis. If all of those things weren't going right, he'd let his teacher know in a way that was not polite. And for some teachers, like Derek, that reality made Allen unlikeable.

That reality raises important questions for any of us who work directly with children. What is it that makes us feel more connection to some students than to others? Is it biases, preconceptions, or cultural preferences? Is it expectations about good versus bad behavior? Is it fear of what others (administrators, colleagues) will think or say if our class looks out of control? In what ways do we define the role of the teacher, and what boundaries separate what we see as our responsibility and what we see as out of our hands? Is it our job to work through the mind-sets and past experiences that inhibit our sense of connection? How much should we care about each other?

> We have to care enough so that all children who are in our classrooms, especially the ones who feel *hardest to like*, know without a doubt that we care about them.

Our answer is that we have to care a lot about all of the children we teach. So much so that the trappings from performance stress to behavioral expectations to cultural superiority are worth examining and overcoming. We have to care enough so that all children who are in our classrooms, especially the ones who *feel* hardest to like, know without a doubt that we care about them.

In the words of Rita Pierson, in her famous TED talk "Every Child Needs a Champion," "Kids don't learn from people they don't like" (2013). Research supports this assertion. Secure relationships with children allow them to safely explore and engage in challenging learning tasks, which improves children's competence and autonomy (Birch and Ladd 1997; Pianta 1999). When students are in caring classroom communities with positive teacher-student relationships, they do better socially and academically (e.g., Finn, Pannozzo, and Achilles 2003; Roorda et al. 2011; Watson and Battistich 2006).

The experience with Allen and many other experiences over the years have led us to believe that when we can focus on specific strategies to build and improve relationships with students, even the ones that seem the most challenging, we can find success with every student. Success doesn't mean perfection, but it does mean recognizing the ways in which every child can and does learn. And these daily successes make a difference—often a life-changing one.

Sadly, we have also come to the conclusion that the opposite is also true. When a teacher dislikes a child, no good can from it. That year is most likely to be a lost one for the child, and when teachers feel that way year upon year, it can lead to even bigger losses.

We've written this book to show why we need to move past our initial reactions to students and act for their best interests as people, not just for the children who do what we say when we say it, not just for the ones who are easy to like, but for the ones who are hardest to understand and connect with. While we can't be responsible for everything that happens in a child's life, we are responsible for how our interactions in the school building make them feel about themselves. We have to learn to appreciate and care for these students. We can't accept that there will be some students each year that we just won't connect with. That can't be defined as our normal. So if that isn't our normal, it's worth examining what is.

Facing the Challenge of Caring for *Every* Child

It is easy to have compassion for students we like. One student who stands out in my mind is Modric. Modric came to our school as a first grader and remained until he graduated from eighth grade. His parents had sent him from a civil war in his homeland to a safer life with a more financially stable aunt and uncle in the United States. He'd come alone; his mother and father, older siblings, and baby twin sisters remained behind. Modric was exceptional—polite, witty, affectionate, hardworking, wide-eyed, and adorable. Every adult loved him. And we loved him even more when we learned that he behaved so exceptionally even though he endured abuse and neglect in his new home. On several occasions, he came to school with open wounds that required numerous stitches. His teeth were rotting to the point of causing severe discomfort that interfered with his eating. His clothes were unwashed. But the staff never hesitated to act. We worked with social workers from his open case through child welfare services and collaborated on support. We did regular home visits. We arranged dental services. We bought him new clothes. By the time he left us, he was safe, healthy, and off to a sought-after high school. It made us feel great to help Modric, and he made it so easy with his resilient, bubbly personality and his darling big brown eyes.

New York Times Magazine's "Ethicist" columnist Randy Cohen has said, "In ethics, cuteness doesn't count" (2009). Yet, for so many of us, the children like Modric, who exhibit cuteness and other desirable qualities, are the ones who get our help, rather than the ones we dislike. But concepts like cuteness and desirable qualities are complex. Cuteness by whose standards? Desirable qualities according to whose cultural norms?

Our relationships with children are often shaped by preconceptions about culture, race, and gender but also sometimes just by what we have been socialized in our own upbringings to expect from them. In my second year of teaching I taught a group of thirty-six fifth and sixth graders chock-full of challenging academic and social needs. In hindsight it was both good and bad to be in this situation so early in my career. I had enough idealism, energy, and creativity to make it positive for most of the students but was green enough to let some students not only slip through the cracks but get kicked out the door, which I either didn't notice or didn't think twice about. Finn was one such student, one of five siblings who had been placed in a foster home. He was in his fifth school in four years because of his many foster home placements, and as I soon found out, his mom took back all of the other siblings except Finn because he was too "difficult." And was he ever. Labeled as "persistently disruptive," he's the only student who ever threatened to kill me (repeatedly), and he got into fights with other students on a daily basis. I empathized with his mom, not him. Of course he was too difficult for her. He was too difficult for any of us. Within weeks, we had started the procedures to have him moved to a self-contained special education classroom at another school.

I now imagine what it must have been like for Finn. Ten years old, just a small child, cast off yet again. Separated from his family, knowing his mother did not want him, bouncing through a series of strange new homes where he might not always have been treated well. Going from school to school where the children were strangers, the teachers unfamiliar, and he found out yet again that he didn't belong. I imagine how alone, terrified, and angry he must have felt.

But, at the time, I didn't think of any of that. The only thing I thought about, as he well knew, was getting rid of him. Within three months of his arrival, he was gone, and I could get to the work that I had defined as my job. At that time, students like Finn were obstacles to be removed, not individuals to whom I was accountable.

It is possible that even with my greatest efforts, my relationship with Finn might never have become truly close, like it was with Modric, and that would be OK. While we might not develop lifelong relationships with every child, we can nurture genuine and consistent relationships that make each student feel safe, supported, and cared for and make ourselves feel competent, knowing that our work has meaning.

Rethinking the Word *Normal*

"It's not *normal* for a teacher to have to deal with this. Our job is to teach the content areas, not to deal with society's problems." How often have you said or heard something like that?

I keep returning to the word *normal* because I hear it all the time. The concept of normal came to us courtesy of a nineteenth-century scientist studying astronomy, Adolphe Quetelet. Quetelet wanted to uncover objective principles of astronomy through identifying averages in measurements (Rose 2016), which he did. He then wondered if he could use the same mathematical concept of averages to identify the ideal in humans and establish expectations for human behavior.

A very appealing concept. Tidy. Predictive. And wrong, especially in regard to human behavior. First, what's average or normal changes. Once women and people of color couldn't vote, gay couples couldn't marry or adopt, and literacy was a privilege of the rich. We're pretty comfortable accepting *normal* as a historical construct, something that changes over long spans of time, but the closer the context comes to our own, the more we sometimes find ourselves using *normal* and *abnormal* to create boundaries between ourselves and those who make us uncomfortable. Of course, identifying behaviors that aren't typical is useful, but not when we're using that information only to judge and dismiss.

When we say the word *normal*, we're categorizing, and when we say, "This isn't normal," to describe one of our students, what we're really saying is that we don't feel up to the challenges presented by that child. Teachers often feel beleaguered because the expectations of their job don't feel normal. And they're not wrong: teacher training doesn't usually live up to the demands of actually being a teacher. Those of us working with kids right now need help getting the tools and understandings we need to be successful today. Let's start by understanding how the makeup of our brains can influence how we view and interact with children.

Examining Our Biases

In classrooms, intentionally or not, we sometimes use students as scapegoats, to allow us to cast off discomfort with ourselves and our practice and to avoid confronting our own weaknesses and insecurities. In Western thought, Hegel described this as the creation of the Other (Kain 1943), or someone who is different from us in some fundamental, lesser, and inferior way, such as values, religion, gender, race, ethnicity, species, or sexuality. The Other is our scapegoat, which in common psychology is the person or people held to blame for a multitude of problems for which they are not responsible. It has roots in ancient religions, in which goats were killed, symbolically carrying away the sins of the community.

Casting children as scapegoats allows us to steal power, to be supreme by saying to some children, "You can't participate; you can't have the rights that some people in this community have; your purpose is to be less than other, more valued members of this community." When we allow for the creation of the Other in our classrooms, we reinforce a pattern of otherness in our society. This pattern of otherness doesn't come from nowhere; it repeats itself because our brains' conceptual networks lean into categorizing. Knowing this can help us correct it.

Changing Entrenched Negative Behaviors

Research has helped us understand that tension exists between two different locations of the brain. Most of us know that our primal brain, the amygdala, generates the immediate response to fear stimuli through fight, flight, or freeze. The amygdala has also emerged as a key region in unconscious-bias research. There are other parts of our brain involved as well, like the prefrontal cortex, which forms impressions and holds memories that cause us to say, "You are either part of my group or part of another."

But we also know that other higher brain functions such as moral reasoning, logic, and critical thinking can override the fear responses and bias and help us to regulate our thoughts and our actions. The brain is the last organ in the human body to fully mature, and as it matures, repeated experiences create new circuitry, or neural pathways, in the brain. Those neural pathways can make our responses harsher or more harmonious—more prone to moral reasoning, logic, and critical thinking.

It is important to know that the pathways, however deeply developed, can be changed again with new repeated experiences. This is called neuroplasticity. We can disrupt and change ingrained behavior patterns—actually physically change the landscape of our brains—by making different choices over a period of time. So the choices we make today and tomorrow and the next day are critical to the choices we make later on. Imagine what we could do for children if we could teach them—not just tell them, but teach them—how to use this information. The body of research on neuroplasticity can help us, and them, expand the choices we make about our own human behavior beyond what it is today (Goleman 1995).

> *It is important to know that the pathways, however deeply developed, can be changed again with new repeated experiences.*

Social and emotional learning is based in part on neuroscience and the belief that through repeated experiences we can help students develop grooves for positive, euphonious ways of interacting in and with the world. The automatic or unconscious responses in our brains can remain thoughts; they do not need to control our actions. If we pause and identify how we feel, we can choose the most constructive action and seek out new information if needed. Too often, we are resistant to new information, to new schema, to a new way of looking at a familiar issue. But it's the act of being in a dialogue about that new stuff that develops our brains, making us more understanding, wiser, and ideally more connected and compassionate people.

There's no such thing as stasis in human development. We are always changing, but we truly learn only when we are willing to examine, discuss, and reflect on these changes. If we're going to take on the responsibility of teaching children, of helping them to see that they are works in progress—and if you are reading this book, you already have—then we have to recognize that we, too, are works in progress and need to live in the stance of learner. When we do that, we begin to open ourselves up to more joyful and fulfilling personal and professional lives.

Children learn behaviors through our intentional and direct teaching as well as through the behaviors we unintentionally model. Because of this, our responsibility for our own behavior is great. We want children to learn to be tolerant, empathetic, and inquisitive and to evolve as learners, thinkers, and people. But all too often, that's not what we teach.

A recent study entitled *Ready to Lead: A National Principal Survey on How Social and Emotional Learning Can Prepare Children and Transform Schools* (DePaoli, Atwell, and Bridgeland 2017) showed that while many believe that teaching children social and emotional competencies is indeed important, there isn't time. Unfortunately, schools rarely take on the work of teaching a child to learn and to grow as a person. In fact, since the introduction of the Common Core State Standards, even fewer educators feel they have time for social and emotional learning (SEL).

Growing into Compassion

Most of us, I think, not only want to develop compassion in our children but would like to believe we embody it ourselves. Daniel Goleman has written about the importance of compassion in being able to connect with others, for personal relationships, for workplace success, and to expand our worldview to include those who may be less fortunate than we are so that we can help. In an interview with Harvard Business Review (May, 2015), Goleman explains, "When you feel compassion, you feel distress when you witness someone else in distress—and because of that you want to help that person."

Compassion comes from the Latin word *compati*, meaning "to suffer with." If you can extend yourself to suffer with someone, it is more likely that you will act on his behalf.

Melanie Joy has written, "The most effective way to distort reality is to deny it; if we tell ourselves there isn't a problem, then we never have to worry about what to do about it. And the most effective way to deny a reality is to make it invisible" (2008, 139).

We are a country that extols diversity, but like that surface-level connection we get through social media, our passion for diversity sits at the surface too. Underneath the surface, we fear difference. If someone's not in our group, it signals danger. Most of our fear is completely irrational and largely unexamined, but it is real nonetheless. We fear difference—ethnic or racial difference, economic difference, sexual-orientation difference, gender difference, religious difference, political difference, and the list goes on. Fear often manifests itself as anger; remember fight, flight, or freeze. Self-awareness is a competency many of us struggle with, so oftentimes, we don't even recognize that a fear response is impacting our behavior, manifesting as anger, and ending up very much in the driver's seat.

With that gap in social and emotional competence (if we aren't self-aware, we can't self-manage very well), we allow fear to block the possibility of connection or compassion and often find ourselves in us-versus-them situations. Whomever we end up against, we put great effort into minimizing their problems and perspectives, and eventually they become invisible to us. They just aren't real enough to deal with. This is a cycle we can stop with a commitment to meeting the fundamental needs of our students and making the time for social and emotional learning.

Recognizing Schools' Institutional Bias

I'd be doing a real injustice to children if I led you to believe that the creation of the Other existed only in the brain. Because of bias, we've created institutions that reflect and enact it on people. This kind of institutionalized othering is called institutional bias. Even if we can't escape it, we can certainly take responsibility for recognizing it and our role in upholding it.

Institutional bias has detrimental effects on a very specific portion of the student population. Data collected by the National Center for Education Statistics in 2012 reveal that students of color made up more than 45 percent of the K–12 student population (Aud et al. 2012). Roughly 80 percent of teachers are white. Whether we have all come to realize it or not, we each bring deep and often unconscious biases, preferences, and cultural norms and expectations with us to the classroom and it plays out for students in very notable ways.

In our country, black children are three times as likely to be suspended as white children. Each of us who works with children bears responsibility for confronting that disparity of treatment between the children who look like most of us and the children who do not. Look at the statistics in the box. What do they say about the bias we carry within ourselves as teachers?

The Oxford Reference website defines *institutional bias* as a "tendency for the procedures and practices of particular institutions to operate in ways which result in certain social groups being advantaged or favored and others being disadvantaged or devalued. This need not be the result of any conscious prejudice or discrimination but rather of the majority simply following existing rules or norms." For example, in a 2015 *New York Times* article analyzing statistical evidence, Sendhil Mullainathan, a professor of economics at Harvard, identified the institutional bias in the disproportionate rate of police killings of black men in America. Here is his take, in brief: Individual police bias might impact the number of killings, but if you somehow removed the individual bias, institutional bias would remain. There would still be suspect descriptions, which overwhelmingly finger black males; police officers are most frequently placed in a neighborhood with more black people; an overwhelming majority of blacks in the United States live in poverty, and there is more violent crime in poverty-stricken neighborhoods, leading to more police interactions; policy often dictates that police officers pursue drug dealers rather than users, and dealers are more often black and users more often not. Individuals are responsible for individual bias. But these structural realities are no more the responsibility of individual police officers than of all of us living in the United States who are either uninformed or informed and choose to look the other way.

If you are asking, "What does this have to do with my work as a teacher?" here is the simple answer: If we don't see the institutional conditions that impede the Other, then we can't understand their experiences or create equitable learning environments for them. If we don't see the institutional conditions that impede

- Black children represent 18 percent of preschool enrollment, but 48 percent of black preschool children receive more than one out-of-school suspension.
- Black students are nearly four times more likely to be suspended and nearly twice as likely to be expelled as white students.
- Black boys are about three times more likely (20 percent) to receive an out-of-school suspension than white boys (6 percent).
- Black girls are six times more likely (12 percent) to receive an out-of-school suspension than white girls (2 percent).

Source: Civil Rights Data Collection (U.S. Department of Education 2016)

children, we are led into misunderstandings that we need to fix students instead of fixing the conditions that marginalize students—and the fixing-children mind-set and teaching-children mind-set oppose each other. As participants in educational institutions, who bring our own biases into the classroom, we need to examine and own our role in maintaining its racist practices.

Cultivating Our Willingness to Help

The reality is, not all children are Modric, and there are plenty of Finns in the classroom mix. There are some students whom, from the moment we meet them, we don't like. There's just something about them that puts us off that we can't quite put our fingers on. Other times, our dislike grows as a particular student challenges us.

The lie "I care about all my students" is similar to the lie "I don't see color." Both statements seek to bury uncomfortable or difficult feelings and make us perpetually ineffective at meeting students' needs. The lie isn't always intentional, as it is one we are socialized to tell. We have grown to believe it as truth, but our behavior often says otherwise.

Every now and then in a planning session, I'll meet a teacher who's bold enough to ask a question that makes everyone else stare into their computer screens as if they haven't heard. "What about the kid who just refuses to get with the program? You know, the one who tells the other kids their mothers suck, who does no work, and whom nothing works for?"

At this point I have a sincere but canned response to such questions: "I don't believe there is a single child whom nothing works for; it's a matter of finding the right approach. And I'd be more than happy to help you think through your future work with that child after this particular meeting ends. If you are willing to try out a few different strategies, I know we will eventually land on the right one."

But no one ever has taken me up on my offer. When we get to the point when we are willing to ask that kind of question out loud, we are without compassion for the child. And that can only mean we have an unhappy teacher and an unhappy student spiraling to a bad place. That can only mean failure on both ends. I've seen that happen enough times to know it well. I've been there myself. But this is the work I am committed to doing, and that I am inviting you to do too, so that none of us remains stuck in such a destructive place.

Planning for students to become people who know they are meaningful members of the school community, who are competent, and who are autonomous requires that we have compassion for each and every student—but especially for the student who is most unlikeable to us. We have all met them, have all taught them, and at times it seems like those children are demanding that we have heroic levels of patience and persistence. We really start to lose it when we realize that patience and persistence are not enough. We can't tolerate it when being who we are in this moment is not enough.

I'm suggesting that we shift our paradigm about how children can and should fit into the structure of a classroom community. Many of us expect children to conform to the model we envision. This often seems like expecting a square peg to fit in a round hole. Just because many children can do it, it doesn't mean everyone should be expected to. Instead we should be thinking about how to make our instruction, both social and academic, conform to student needs.

> *As we better understand our own social and emotional needs, we can analyze more deeply why we react as we do to challenging students.*

Our book lays out multiple pathways for you to show students that you care, through revisions to current practice. The path you take depends on what your students need and what you feel ready to take on. To start, we have to become aware of how we're feeling about these students and wrestle with those feelings, however uncomfortable they are. Without that step, we won't have the motivation to go further. That's why we've created space for you to explore why denying your negative feelings works against your students and the work you do with them, and we offer specific strategies for reflecting on how you really feel about students.

We also have to develop more knowledge and understanding of these children and ourselves. As we better understand our own social and emotional needs, we can analyze more deeply why we react as we do to challenging students. Further, understanding how these needs influence students and their behavior helps us better understand them and make a plan for helping them.

We can use all this to analyze specifically what is going on between us and our students. We explore some of the reasons some children are so much harder for us to like than others. Again, confronting some of these truths, like the fact that we bring a host of biases with us into our classrooms, can be challenging, but it is necessary if we are going to make a change.

Finally, we have to figure out what to do with all these newfound feelings and knowledge! We'll help you learn how to actively develop compassion for these students. We'll also set out strategies for how to see them as more lovable by meeting their basic needs for competence, relatedness, and autonomy.

Taking on the challenges this book addresses takes courage and hard work. As with most aspects of teaching, there is no one right answer, no magic bullet. But we are confident that the discomfort you might feel as you read this book and examine your feelings and the struggles you encounter as you try to understand these students and how to help them will be worth it. Gradually, you will begin to see changes in yourself and your students that will allow you to be a compassionate and effective teacher for all students. As we say later in the book about children, we say to you now: We have high expectations of you. We believe you have the capacity to make others feel better than they feel right now. Figure 0.1 shows some ways to accomplish that. Now go to it.

{commitment}

Track Disciplinary Practices

Keep track:

Choose a two-week period of time where you will record all of your "disciplinary actions" and the children involved. These include classroom removals, phone calls home, loss of privileges, reprimands, or whatever you do in your classroom to give consequences.

Reflect:

What do you notice about the children involved? Are there any patterns along race, gender, income, or other identity lines?

Synthesize:

What have you realized from this exercise that you didn't realize before? Are there any implications for what you might do differently?

Notes:

Figure 0.1

01

Your Feelings Matter

{ difficulty }

Juan Felt Disliked

When I was teaching, a parent at a parent-teacher conference shared that her child, Juan, felt that I didn't like him and picked on him. My immediate reaction was shock and denial. After all, I prided myself on being a kind and caring teacher. I had spent years investigating the social-emotional realm and worked hard to foster positive relationships with all of my students. It didn't help that the conference concerned the child's academic struggles and the parent was unhappy to hear about those. It would have been easy to dismiss the complaint about not liking the child as the parent's way of avoiding a challenging topic or trying to put the blame for the academic problems on me.

But the comment stuck in the back of my mind, and in the days following the conference, I began to notice that there might be a grain of truth in what the child and his parent had said. I used metacognition as a strategy for attending to what Juan's parent had brought to my attention:

➔ I tried to pay attention to what I was feeling and what was happening with the child and to see things from his point of view. Almost immediately, I sensed something was off with how I treated him. I felt uncomfortable with this discovery but forced myself to keep noticing.

➔ I started to pay more attention to the anxiety I was feeling as a result of Juan's lack of academic progress. My principal put a lot of pressure on all of us to bring children up to or above grade level, and I too believed that it was imperative that all students succeed. I put enormous pressure on myself when he and others did not seem to make progress. I began to notice that some of my anxiety might sound like frustration to Juan when he failed to remember things that he previously seemed to have learned or struggled to move forward.

➔ I realized that because he was frequently late to class, I didn't know this child as well as some of my other students and didn't chat with him as much about his interests and experiences. I wondered if, from his point of view, this might be a sign of me not liking him.

➔ I also realized that I was somewhat put off by Juan's lack of grooming. I wondered if this might have unconsciously been translated into me keeping my distance from him. His clothes were frequently unwashed and he suffered from frequent lice outbreaks—as a result, I think I was more standoffish with him than with other students.

Slowly I began to recognize that my feelings toward Juan were more complicated than I had originally thought and that although I did like him, I might not feel as positively as I had thought. He certainly might have felt disliked. I began to see the negative effects of my unrecognized feelings.

If asked, we might claim that we care for all of our students. We like to think we're fair and treat them all equally. But, as we discussed in the introduction, we all experience negative emotions toward children. Experiencing these feelings isn't the problem, though; the problem is failing to recognize our feelings or, worse, failing to do anything about them when we do. When we let our emotions go unchecked, either by failing to be aware of them or not doing anything about them, we treat children about whom we feel negatively differently and worse than other children. We teach them differently too. These actions have consequences, often dire, for these students. It is crucial that we stay on top of how we feel and then take action.

Recognize the Impact
of Your Negative Feelings

The short-term effects for students toward whom we feel uncomfortable, hostile, or otherwise negatively are many and include deteriorated peer relationships, internalization of negative messages, poor academic performance, and increased negative behavior.

Diminished Peer Relationships

As you've likely experienced in your teaching, children often pick up on our words and cues. On the positive side, we sometimes hear them helping their classmates with academic work, using the same words we used in the lesson. Or we overhear them encouraging a classmate with the same tone and phrases we use. On the other hand, this phenomenon often means children treat classmates they see us ignoring, scoffing at, speaking harshly to, or treating with sarcasm in the same way. Remember the scapegoat? The creation of the Other? Peers are even more likely to do this if they share our negative feelings toward a child. Our actions can give them the green light to treat certain children more harshly or disrespectfully than they do others. Or we might actually influence them to develop negative feelings that didn't exist before. As a result, children who already have considerable obstacles to forming positive peer relationships have yet another put in their way when we fail to wrestle with and reverse our negative feelings about them.

With Juan, I began to wonder whether other children were picking up on my own feelings about him. I saw them keeping a respectful but still present distance from him. I had to wonder if they were unconsciously following my lead. Whether we like it or not, we are often children's role models for how to treat each other.

Internalization of Negative Messages

Another result of our disparate treatment of certain children is that they internalize the messages we are sending, developing negative feelings about themselves and their capabilities. A great deal of research shows the negative and often debilitating effects of self-loathing and low self-esteem. It is hard for children like Juan to believe in themselves when they feel that their teachers don't. I began to wonder whether at least some of his academic struggles resulted from the negative messages I was sending him.

Poor Academic Performance

Children who lack positive relationships with their teachers simply don't perform as well academically as those who have good relationships with their teachers. The reasons for this are complicated, but one reason might be that we don't provide as much academic support for students with whom we have little affinity. We might also not provide support in as effective a way as they need. The children's internalization of our and others' negative treatment of them can also prevent them from effectively taking in whole-class instruction or channeling the help we give them.

Again, as Rita Pierson (2013) expressed, children don't learn from people they don't like. A close relationship with a teacher allows students to safely explore and engage in challenging learning tasks (Birch and Ladd 1997; Pianta 1999). Students, including those with diagnosed behavior disorders, report that their most effective teachers established caring relationships with them (Hoy and Weinstein 2006).

Juan was in a small tutoring group I held, and I began to notice that while I could be impatient with Juan's lack of progress, I had enormous patience for another child in that group who was even further behind grade level than Juan. I heard the encouraging words I offered to Angel and wondered whether I offered enough of those to Juan. What was he to make of the difference in treatment? Once again, I had to question whether I was unconsciously standing in the way of some of his academic progress.

Increased Rule Breaking or Negative Behaviors

Children with poor relationships with their teachers are also less likely to follow classroom norms and more likely to openly defy them. When teachers establish positive relationships with children, they do better socially and academically (e.g., Patrick et al. 2003; Roorda et al. 2011; Watson and Battistich 2006).

If they were already generally uncooperative when they came into the class, they might become more so. If they have a tendency to be defiant, they might defy us even more frequently. This phenomenon can begin a dangerous cycle—as our negativity fosters negative behaviors, we find the children even more frustrating and annoying, we treat them more negatively, and they react in kind.

Often for the same reasons we have trouble with a child, the colleagues teaching that child before and after us do also. Sometimes we magnify this possibility by broadcasting to the child's next teachers to expect trouble from this child. As we discuss in Section 3, there might be valid reasons for talking negatively about a student. However, telling other teachers this child is impossible is not valid, and we do it to help relieve ourselves of the tremendous guilt or pressure we can feel from having failed with him or her. But years of poor relationships with teachers, combined with underlying causes such as trauma or neglect outside of school, can lead to long-term negative effects for students.

A Pattern of Failure

As you might expect, years of negative experiences with teachers and classmates at school have lasting effects. Students who are suspended are more likely to be suspended again, more likely to be expelled, and more likely to not complete high school. Students' experience of being treated negatively, especially when compounded by internalization of those feelings, can also diminish their relationships at school and when seeking work. Without a solid footing academically or socially, it is not surprising that many of these students struggle to find and keep jobs. Conversely, students who are "better behaved"—meaning they exhibit social and emotional competence—perform better academically (e.g., Coolahan et al. 2000; Graziano et al. 2007; Hughes et al. 2008; Klem and Connell 2004; Normandeau and Guay 1998; Wentzel 1993), have higher graduation rates from high school, and have better employment opportunities (Blum and Libbey 2004; Greenberg et al. 2003).

{ strategy }

Evaluate Your Emotions

As I had to do with Juan, sometimes it helps to step back and analyze whether you are struggling with negative feelings about any children. One way to do this is to take out your class list, look at the names, and consider your emotional reactions. It can help to pay attention to these emotions in particular:

- anger
- anxiety
- disgust
- fear
- extreme annoyance
- hopelessness or a sense of failure
- resentment

When we start to feel any of these emotions, we need to stop and take a few minutes to analyze what is going on. I can't emphasize enough how important it is to let yourself feel what you feel. Don't censor yourself when you're alone. Instead, listen to your internal thinking, notice it, and be curious about it. See Figure 1.1. As discussed in the introduction, our feelings are signals to us that either something is going right or it isn't. What marks us as mature adults and responsible professionals is choosing how we behave once we have discovered what is causing our feelings.

{ commitment }

Shift to Empathy

Remember:

Think of a child you are teaching now or have taught recently, one you feel especially challenged by. Try to picture that child and a troubling interaction you had. Remember what you were feeling, the thoughts that went through your head, the parts of your body where you felt stress, or fear, or any other emotions that might have occurred. With that child and that event fresh in your mind, investigate your empathy using the questions below.

Reflect:

- *Cognitive empathy:* Can you understand the child's point of view? How might he see the situation? What might he be thinking? Can you identify why he might feel angry, distant, disengaged, or defiant?

- *Emotional empathy:* Can you feel what the child is feeling? Are you able to imagine yourself in her shoes?

- *Empathetic concern:* Can you figure out what the child needs from you to help make the situation better? What steps could you take to improve your relationship with the child, to help him feel in control of his life, or to help him feel competent?

Notes:

continues

Reflect: *continued*

- *Compassion:* Do you feel enough distress for the child that you are willing to change your actions to make things better for her? Are you willing to move beyond caring and do something different to help? (Goleman 2015)

Notes:

Synthesize:

What new understanding do you have about yourself? About the child?

Figure 1.1

Although every child and situation is unique, it can also be helpful to consider some common characteristics of students with whom many teachers struggle. You can use Figure 1.2 to help you do this.

CHILDREN FOR WHOM WE MIGHT HAVE NEGATIVE EMOTIONS

Students who challenge us or make us feel less competent or in control, for example, those who

- express views we find offensive (such as racism, genderism, or misogyny)
- make us look bad, for example, in front of our colleagues or administrators
- explode—lose their temper or have extreme outbursts when upset
- frequently and defiantly refuse to follow directions or classroom norms
- correct us or point out our mistakes often
- seem to ignore or won't follow directions
- have parents who frequently complain about us or their child's school experience
- are part of a race, religion, or other group we have implicit or explicit bias against

Students we have a hard time trusting, such as those who

- blurt out or say inappropriate things (profanity, insults to other people, sexual talk)
- steal or hoard things
- are sneaky
- deface property

continues

CHILDREN FOR WHOM WE MIGHT HAVE NEGATIVE EMOTIONS *continued*

Students who have unseemly habits or appearance, such as those who

- regularly smell bad
- are extremely dirty
- frequently pick their nose
- touch their privates
- urinate or defecate in inappropriate places

Students who hurt classmates, for example, those who

- get physical with or threaten other students
- are mean to other students
- frequently tell on other children
- bully other people

Students who seem disengaged from school, such as those who

- are withdrawn
- don't seem to care about learning or school
- repeatedly rebuff our efforts to help or get to know them
- are hyperactive or easily distracted
- behave like the class clown

Students who seem to think they are better than others, for example, those who

- appear to feel extremely entitled
- flaunt their wealth

Figure 1.2

{ strategy }

Value Student and Family Feedback

It is possible that you have read the preceding chart and told yourself that there's no need for reflection—you've behaved fine with students. You might feel that any negative response has been appropriate and was in the best interest of the student or of the class as a whole. If you are thinking that, we ask you to pause and reflect again. All of us have erred in our interactions with students, and creating the space to see it and name it allows us to make shifts in our future relationships.

Too often, our words and our actions communicate that a child should feel self-loathing. It is often not what we intend or are conscious of. What we want is for the child to understand and have a model for better behavior, to choose constructive action. What we don't recognize is that children need explicit modeling, strategies, and opportunities to practice this over time in order to achieve it.

As our opening story shows, it can be tempting to dismiss a child's complaints ("You pick on me," "You don't like me," "You're unfair") or a parent's concerns ("My child doesn't feel comfortable in your classroom," "My kid has anxiety about coming to school," "You pick on my child"). Often you might even have a good reason for being tempted to do so. If the child or parent presents his concerns rudely, angrily, or as a personal attack, we naturally feel threatened and defensive. In that posture, it's hard to take a sober look at what the child or parent is saying. Sometimes as well we get the sense that the parent or child is trying to use statements like this to manipulate us into changing our behavior, for example, around discipline.

But we should see these claims, however unartfully presented, as the red flags they are. If we can rise above our defensiveness, step back, and reflect, we can see that they often contain at least a kernel of truth. See Figure 1.3 for some suggestions to make this shift.

{ commitment }

Take the Family's or Child's Point of View

When you can sense yourself feeling attacked or defensive, try to consider things *from the point of view of the family or child*. Think about the most recent time this has occurred. Try to stretch your thinking to answer the following questions:

	Notes:
Is it possible you have, however unconsciously, appeared to be unfair?	
Is it possible you have some negative feelings toward the child and have shown those?	
Is it possible you're singling her out in some way?	

Figure 1.3

Invite a Trusted Colleague
to Observe

Almost all of us strive to be fair and balanced and treat students equally. But, in reality, we sometimes fall short of that goal. It can be hard to see that ourselves, and as much as we would like to think it doesn't, implicit bias influences our behavior. As administrators and coaches, both of us have been in classrooms and seen teachers repeatedly correct one child for a behavior, such as interrupting, while simultaneously allowing other children to do that same behavior; giving positive feedback to most children while repeatedly finding fault, often trivial, with others; and using questions or sarcasm to put a child down. When we talked with teachers afterward, most were completely unaware of these issues. If you have a colleague you trust, ask that person to come sit in your classroom for a period and watch how you are doing with treating all students with respect and dignity. It takes courage to do this and hear the results, but often a colleague's fresh eyes can help you uncover problems and emotions you didn't even know you had.

{ strategy }

Videotape Yourself

Particularly if you are beginning to suspect that you have some negative feelings for a child or that the child thinks so, videotape yourself in action. Watch yourself teaching and analyze it through the lens of the child. Watch for the following clues:

→ *Facial expressions:* From a child's point of view, could you be frequently frowning for no reason, glowering, or avoiding eye contact? As you think about your facial expressions, consider that children who have experienced abuse or trauma can be extremely sensitive to changes in facial expression.

→ *Number of contacts with children:* If you rarely or never make contact with a child, that can be a sign of a problem. On the other hand, you might also look for the other extreme. Watch for whether you are frequently correcting one child for a behavior but ignoring similar behaviors when other students exhibit them.

→ *Words and tone:* Look for increased sarcasm, harshness, dismissive-ness, and quick assumptions made toward one child. Also consider whether you would be comfortable having a principal, a colleague, a friend, or the child's parent hear the tone you use with one or more children.

{strategy}

Keep Track of Your Interactions with Students

Find some way to keep track of your interactions with students. You might, for instance, keep a simple T-chart of positive and negative interactions you have with a student you are struggling with during a short period of your day (see the Attention Log in Figure 1.4 for an example). Or, if you are beginning to suspect some negative emotions, you might just journal or reflect at the end of the day about what happened with that child during the day.

We know from experience how hard it can be to acknowledge or wrestle with negative feelings. These feelings can make us feel like bad teachers or failures. Especially if we don't know what to do next, they can leave us feeling hopeless as well. But if we don't admit the feelings are there or just excuse them by saying it happens with some kids, the consequences for the students are dire. It is critical that we not live either in denial or in acceptance of our negative feelings toward children but instead acknowledge them, try to understand the cause of them, and do something about them.

ATTENTION LOG

One-Hour Log: Minh

Positive	Negative
8:30 Good morning/handshake. Talked about show he watched last night. *9:25* Reading conference. Great job tracking character change over time.	*9:05* Corrected to sit still on carpet. *9:07* Stop talking. *9:13* Stop talking. *9:15* Stop touching. *9:16* Sent to seat. *9:19* Stop tapping at desk.

Figure 1.4

What Children Need

{ difficulty }

Willy Was Marked by Trauma

Willy, a fifth grader, faced many challenges at home. These included lacking a safe environment and the necessary support and resources to succeed. He bore the scar of having been burned with a hot iron on his arm. Teachers at the school were aware of his situation but not sensitive to his needs. Because he came to school in unwashed clothes every day and carried an odor of not having bathed, children would routinely try to sit as far away from him as they could. Teachers would say, "You have Willy this year? Good luck with that." Eleven-year-old Willy spent most of his school day in a corner, rocking and mumbling under his breath. Behind academically, Willy seemed to put most of his attention on stealing and hoarding food. When children complained that their lunches and snacks were missing, the food could usually be found in Willy's bulging jacket.

As Willy's teacher, I wasn't really sure what to do for him. I'd made the necessary mandated reports, made some phone calls home, and even tried a few home visits, but despite my efforts, he remained the only child whose parents I never met. So I started with what I believed I could control, the one immediate thing I could do to help. I made sure the rest of the class didn't ostracize him. No students would be allowed to treat any other student like a pariah. By the time I taught Willy, I had learned that every child had to feel like he or she belonged there. While I wasn't perfect at it, I had a set of strategies that I used consistently, such as

→ having daily morning meetings where students shared in numerous ways about their interests, families, and culture;

→ allowing students to choose the topics they would write about;

→ inviting families in for monthly celebrations;

→ reading books and studying topics that would reflect student identities and interests;

→ taking lots of field trips, both work- and play-related, to spend out-of-classroom time together so we would get to know each other as people; and

→ allowing—as my former principal had recently reminded me, much to the custodian's dismay—all children to hand-paint the chairs and parts of the walls so the classroom really felt like it was theirs.

In addition to these steps I took for all children, I took specific steps to support Willy as well. I made sure that Willy was secure in having extra snacks to take home but did it discreetly so that the rest of the class wouldn't be resentful. I decided to have a conversation with my class without Willy there, so I could be very clear with them about my expectations for how we would treat him and take care of each other. It felt necessary at the time to do this in order to protect him, since he had a reputation that followed him from previous years in the school, and they'd witnessed him being treated as an outcast and had perhaps even participated in that behavior. In hindsight and with knowledge I've gained over the years, I realize now that he might have felt like a more important part of the community if I had had this conversation with him present and allowed him to witness the genuine willingness of his peers to be there for him. His inclusion in the conversation could have built upon the safe learning environment I was trying to create, where students would respect the multiple identities that existed in the classroom.

While I couldn't be sure of their previous participation, I could be sure that nine-, ten-, and eleven-year-olds could understand that Willy's behavior was a sign that things weren't happy or comfortable for him. We had to prove to him that we weren't going to make things worse and that maybe we could make things better. You might think this worked because that particular group of children was kind, but I've never taught children—ever—who when asked and expected to didn't rise to such an occasion with kindness and grace. Every student can always be taught and expected to

→ greet classmates in the morning and say goodbye at the end of the day;

→ smile and make eye contact;

→ ask an alone student to sit with him or her at lunch, play at recess, join a work group, or partner up; and

→ take the initiative and go sit next to an alone student during instruction, lunch, or work time.

Although at the time I was acting on instinct, I now understand why that went so well. When children are asked to be thoughtful of others and we give them the tools and expectation to meet that request, we also give them a sense of social and emotional competence. In the asking, we are saying to students, "I have high expectations of you. I believe you have the capacity to make others feel better than they feel right now. Here are some ways to accomplish that. Now go to it." The opportunity to try out being their best selves gives power to children. So, by instinct and accident, the students in my classroom learned to be capable of including Willy. And the actions of his classmates helped Willy begin to recognize that he could be someone that others wanted to be around. For anyone, but especially an outsider like Willy, being included builds not only relatedness but also competence. Willy came to feel not only that he was part of the group but that he belonged because he was capable of making connection.

As a teacher, I was learning to articulate and teach what children need and what we and our classroom and school community are responsible to give them:

1. **Students should feel like they belong in their classroom communities.** *They should know that their teachers and peers want them there and that they are important members of the community.*

2. **Students should feel socially, emotionally, and academically competent.** *They should know and feel like they are good at multiple things. For example, I'm good at greeting people in the morning and making them smile; I'm a good editor; I'm a good mathematician; I'm good at getting to work right away and being productive; or I'm good at including others on the playground.*

3. **Students should feel autonomous.** *They should understand and manage the multiple ways and times that they get to make decisions for themselves. These decisions might include what to make or study as a writer, what book to read, where to sit to read, and whether or not work alone or with peers.*

And yet overlooking these basic needs—for all children, not just extreme cases like Willy—is too common.

All of us, no matter how good we are as teachers, sometimes have to work against a deficit model when we meet a particularly challenging student and sometimes even when we don't. Implicit bias based on race, class, gender, and perceptions of disability are so deeply embedded in our cultural fabric that we don't even realize we are seeing human variations as deficits that result in low expectations for students. These low expectations characterize a deficit model, which at its core means we define children based on perceived weaknesses rather than strengths.

There is a very clear and well-researched danger in this for children, especially for children of color and low-income children. Teacher expectations for such students are lower than for their affluent white counterparts (Aud et al. 2012). To compound the issue, findings also show that low teacher expectations are more of a predictor of student success than student motivation (DeMonte and Hanna 2014).

{ shift }

Focus on Assets, Not Deficits

An asset model focuses on what unique cultural capital, skills, or interests children bring with them. Figure 2.1 shows some language choices that reflect how we see a child. Note that the examples here describe Willy. Notice the power of shifting our language from a deficit model to an asset model.

	SHIFTING FROM A DEFICIT MODEL TO AN ASSET MODEL FOR WILLY		
	Willy	**Deficit Model**	**Asset Model**
COMPETENCIES	Relationships with peers	Ignores and avoids contact with peers, but at times can be verbally explosive.	Shy and hesitant initially but willing to engage with peers with genuine invitations and wait time. Responds to sincerity and space. Sometimes giggles when being asked for or receiving advice during conferences. Appears to be delighted at genuine peer attention.
	Decision making	Incapable of making decisions. Always chooses opposition or inaction.	Is supported by a consistent offering of small, manageable decisions. Takes on more decision making with each success.

continues

	SHIFTING FROM A DEFICIT MODEL TO AN ASSET MODEL FOR WILLY *continued*	
Willy	**Deficit Model**	**Asset Model**
Relationships with teacher	Tunes out teacher directions. Avoids eye contact and one-on-one inter-actions. Mumbles and rocks during instruction.	Works hard to attend to the teacher but works best when allowed to keep a physical distance during whole-class instruction. Takes and applies feedback when given appropriate time to think about and apply it. Is private, so offers personal information in small doses.
Academic competence	Extremely low pro-ductivity. Appears to struggle with or avoid all academic work. Avoids all group work.	Enjoys short and familiar tasks. Makes creative changes or builds skill with each repetition of a task. Willing to give every task a try.

COMPETENCIES

Figure 2.1

While it's essential to do this kind of reflection, it's just as important to think about creating and maintaining the conditions where school becomes a place where all students are seen and appreciated for their assets—one where that experience is so positive that they become motivated participants. Relatedness, competence, and autonomy are the critical factors in both motivation and engagement to become self-determined individuals, and the absence of these factors can lead to a detrimental effect on individuals (Deci and Ryan 1985). Helping students realize these traits should be our goal every day and in every lesson throughout every school year. When we have authentic high expectations for students, and we create the conditions in which they can become motivated and engaged, we are creating an optimal environment for their success.

Recently, I was coaching a group of teachers to plan their first units of study for the school year in reading and writing. There was lots of talk about reading and writing standards, and the teachers were eager to jump to lessons and activities that met the standards, but I asked that they put those details on hold for a minute. I needed their unit planning to be informed by a more foundational question: *How is what is happening in my classroom each day supporting children's sense of belonging, social and academic competence, and autonomy?*

Relatedness, competence, and autonomy: these are the three fundamental psychological needs all humans share. Without feelings of relatedness, competence, or autonomy, we don't—we can't—live fulfilling lives. And yet so many children who pass through the doors of schools never have these needs met. In the largest student survey prior to 2009, researchers found that only 48 percent of grades 6–12 students felt teachers cared about them as individuals (Quaglia Institute for Student Aspirations 2008). Only 45 percent felt teachers cared if they were absent from school. Meeting these needs for children has to become central to our work, and we have to model for children what it looks like to be someone who values meeting those needs.

It is a challenge to ensure that each child feels relatedness, competence, and autonomy. And that makes sense. Each child is different and has unique needs. In Figure 2.2, I've listed some key qualities or behaviors that a teacher who values meeting the fundamental needs of students might have. These are the same qualities or behaviors we might need to demonstrate to other adults (parents, colleagues, loved ones) or experience ourselves in order to meet each other's needs.

Need	Ways to Meet the Needs of Children	What This Might Sound Like
RELATEDNESS	• Make consistent efforts to connect with all students. • View differences as assets rather than deficits. • Know students personally and academically. • Put yourself in the shoes of others in order to understand their experience.	• "Get ready for morning meeting. Patrick is going to lead the greeting today." • "For tomorrow's share, it will be Fanta's, Olivia's, and Charis' turns. We are going to tell about something we love to do with someone from our lives we care about. They will take three questions or comments at each turn." • "Today I'll eat lunch at John's table, and you can decide what the lunch talk will be about." • "You seem really upset. Can you tell me about what happened and what you are feeling? I might ask questions, not because I think you are wrong, but just because I want to understand better."

MEETING THE NEEDS OF CHILDREN

continues

Need	Ways to Meet the Needs of Children	What This Might Sound Like
COMPETENCE	• Listen closely to what children do or say and name it positively. • Reinforce significant strengths in even small accomplishments. • Help children develop systems for staying organized. • Recognize what children know and can do and help them build a scaffold to new learning.	• "So what you are saying is . . . It sounds like you are . . ." • "I see that you got your book out right away. Good job getting started. In a few minutes, once everyone is reading, I'd love to hear how you like it so far." • "Remember, the blue folder is where your math papers go; the green folder is for writing drafts." • "I see that you have started to add into your draft 'he grumbled,' and 'he whispered.' It seems like you are thinking about the words *he grumbled* and *whispered*, but you don't have it here yet. How about we work on adding in that dialogue in one or two places? I'll show you how."

continues

Need	Ways to Meet the Needs of Children	What This Might Sound Like
AUTONOMY	• Give children opportunities to choose work, materials, assignments, or peers to work with. • Ask children to self-reflect and assess experiences. • Allow space for behavioral mistakes and revision. • Create ongoing opportunities to critique social and social justice issues.	• "I see you are almost done with your book. What are you thinking of reading next? Will that be on your own or with a partner?" • "What strategies did you use to complete that? What was most or least helpful?" • "You have your presentation criteria and all your research done. I'm trusting you two to be ready to present on Thursday." • "Do you agree with the character's decision to . . . ? How would you have handled it? Where do you see things like this happening in real life? How do you feel about it?"

Figure 2.2

{ strategy }

Assess Children's
Self-Perceived Agency

However much we do to meet students' needs, it is not enough to stop there. It is always important to understand how children perceive their experience in school. What follows in Figure 2.3 is a tool you can use for all students or for those you are most concerned about, formally or conversationally. If some students in your class feel their needs aren't being met, then they probably aren't. These kinds of data can help you shift your practice in ways that will be most meaningful to children.

ASSESS STUDENTS' AGENCY		
Relatedness	**Competence**	**Autonomy**
☐ At school I feel like I am part of a group. ☐ I can talk with others in school about things that really matter to me. ☐ Some of my closest relationships are with people at school. ☐ I am close to children and adults at school. ☐ People care about me at school.	☐ I am good at many of the things I do at school. ☐ I can manage most of my tasks at school. ☐ I feel like I can complete difficult jobs at school. ☐ There are things I can help others with at school. ☐ Adults and children know the things I am good at.	☐ I can act like myself at school. ☐ The work at school is the work I want to be doing. ☐ At school I can choose to do my work in the way I think I can do it best. ☐ I can make plans about what work I want to do, how long it will take, whom I do it with, and how to do it. ☐ Adults and children trust me to get things done.

Figure 2.3

Peter Senge, who wrote *The 5th Discipline* (1990), describes what he calls a "shift-the-burden archetype" as a way to illustrate that treating symptoms, rather than identifying and fixing fundamental problems, can lead to a further dependence on symptomatic solutions. We see the symptoms of a problem, and instead of digging deeply to identify the root cause and address that, we attack the symptom. A medical example might be that an athlete has lower back pain, so she relies on anti-inflammatory medications to mask the pain and returns to normal activity. Then there's the unintended side effect. The athlete doesn't know that a small tear in a muscle has been causing the pain, and the return to normal activity will cause such disruption that surgery will be required, and the same level of activity might never be possible again.

We see this in schools all the time.

I remember working with middle school students who suffered from personal trauma—living in poverty, having a parent in prison, and having the burden of caring for themselves and younger siblings. They were so carefully managed (and controlled) by adults, both behaviorally and academically, that they received full scholarships to private boarding schools. The adults were shifting the burden, not dealing with the trauma. With a change in settings and the absence of careful management, the students were soon engaged in behavior that led to expulsion (an unintended side effect).

We see this too with schools. Imagine the teacher who is in danger of losing his job because of poor standardized test scores, which are a result of his lack of both support and personal development as an educator as well as how the school itself fails to support high-poverty, high-trauma students behaviorally or academically throughout their entire school experience. The teacher both teaches solely to the test and fudges some answers on the score sheet (shifting the burden). The unintended side effects are many.

The underlying belief that creates these problems? That expectations must be applied and adhered to without exception. But *reasons* for student behavior or achievement are not excuses. Educators must become experts at finding out the *reasons* not only for misbehavior but for lack of growth, for lack of progress, or for a child or an adult who is struggling within a school. Otherwise, we focus on symptomatic solutions, which causes other problems. Instead, we need to look at the root cause. Like doctors, who would not routinely treat all fevers without an understanding of why the fevers existed as a symptom, we can't continue to blindly accept blanket responses to school-based problems.

{ strategy }

Value Approximation

What if we looked at problems as signals to us that we were not creating the appropriate conditions for children to approximate something before they got it right? In our earliest development, we learn to talk, to read, and to write through approximations. Brian Cambourne has often reminded us of early language development as a classic example of celebrated approximations. A young child's first sounds often are so far removed from a word—a single letter sound perhaps—but we react with glee, eye contact, and applause, saying back a word *we think but aren't certain* she was attempting to say. Positive feedback and correct and frequent examples of language use around a toddler lead to language acquisition. Giving negative feedback, telling children they are wrong, and making corrections do not lead children to be language users, and yet those are moves we rely on once children reach school age. We must remember that no matter how old we are, having repeated opportunities to approximate new skills, strategies, and behaviors is critical to our learning and development and will continue to be throughout our lives. Through approximation, we can become better teachers, and we can help children meet the important needs of relatedness, competence, and autonomy (Cambourne 2002).

Even for those who are incredibly sophisticated in their practice, approximations are critical to learning. Scientists and mathematicians use approximations to experiment, theorize, and create new laws or understandings. At its simplest, it might mean using a rounded number for a calculation before deciding on the exact formula or an exact answer. Or it might be approximating the shape of a planet as a sphere as a starting point before determining its precise or accurate shape.

As teachers we're always approximating toward the ideal. In some moments, we hit the mark, while we miss it in others, never perfectly consistent because we're human beings. Reflection on our own attempts, successes, and struggles is essential to our learning so that our professional lives can always be reaching toward a closer approximation of our ideal of teaching, our ideal relationships with children. We have to live this model ourselves to honor it in children's growth and learning.

In classrooms, we often neglect the value of approximation. Approximation creates the necessary space between the introduction of an idea and the expectation that it will be realized with perfection. Remember the deficit and asset table (pages 36–37)?

Willy did best when given space—both physical and mental—to accept invitations to learning and to relationships. He needed repetition and the experience of giving something many celebrated tries.

The class' behavior toward Willy might have softened his edge a bit, but he was still a recluse. Much of the day he remained in the farthest corner of the classroom, rocking and mumbling. From time to time, he'd venture in closer during our meeting times on the carpet, and that was progress. He was always listening though. One day, several months into the school year, a near miracle happened. The class was studying poetry in reading and writing, and on this day, we were discussing William Carlos Williams' poem "This Is Just to Say," an intimate, twenty-eight word poem, said to be written as a note to his wife, in which the writer confesses to having eaten the plums that were sitting in the icebox.

I could see it was piquing Willy's interest, but it wasn't until students went off to write that I saw him acting completely differently. He was *writing*! For days, Willy worked through dozens of variations on this poem, and he willingly shared them with the class. "I have eaten the potato chips which were on the counter, which you were probably saving for lunch. Forgive me, they were delicious, so crisp and so salty. . . ." Willy's food-stealing experiences made him connect with this poem, and he saw that William Carlos Williams made it a safe subject for him to write about. To this day, the experience feels serendipitous, as if I'd actually stumbled upon something that worked. And while to some extent I did, I didn't know this poem would be the lever, but the groundwork the class and I had laid with Willy awakened something in him that made it possible for there to even be a lever. We awakened the possibility of his competence.

All of us, the students and I, were so proud of his new participation and passion, and we sure let him know it. "Willy," a child would say, "I really like the way you described potato chips. The crispness and the saltiness are the most important things about them." And, "Willy, did the person forgive you for taking them?" We treated his newfound identity as a writer and as a poet with the utmost seriousness and utmost celebration, in the same spirit as a parent would treat a child's new language accomplishment as he learned to speak in sentences. Willy was having the experience of feeling competent, not because of directives but because the conditions were right for him.

Part of giving Willy the experience of autonomy meant giving him space. I'd seen other staff get into battles with him that they couldn't win, where they had tried to impose their will on a child that clearly had a stronger will than any of us.

Over years, he'd developed behaviors to create space for himself. Forcing him to sit closer, to stop rocking, to stop mumbling, to write more, to do what everyone else was doing might have on the surface made it appear as if we were doing our jobs as teachers. In reality, I could see that when others tried that approach, it only created more distance between them and him.

Sometimes we think there are two options with children: forcing or ignoring. Imposing our will or throwing our hands up in despair. But autonomy exists in the choices in between, and so with Willy, I lingered there. I gave him consistent invitations to move in closer, to try things out, to make decisions for himself. Sometimes to approximate and sometimes to not quite hit the mark on approximation. I made sure to let him know that I saw him, I recognized his choices, and I would remember to follow up with new invitations should he decline the current ones. Ultimately, the decisions had to be his own. And ultimately, he did start making more of them.

Life isn't a fairy tale, so I won't pretend everything was perfect for Willy after that, but he made so much progress socially and academically. He was a reader and a writer with a unique identity. He became someone important and valued in the community. And I learned I could be the kind of teacher who could continue to evolve in order to support a child like Willy and make him feel safe and successful in my classroom. See Figure 2.4 for some suggestions to examine your own practices of labeling students.

{commitment}

Examine Asset and Deficit Labeling

Remember:

If we want to catch ourselves when we have low expectations, it's worth taking multiple looks at students who feel challenging to us. Select a child, perhaps the same one you thought about in Section 1, and remember what that child behaved like and what you expected of that child. Describe the child based on the four categories below. Be as precise as possible in your written descriptions. Then think about how you felt during those times and even how you feel now while remembering.

	What have you observed?	Is this asset- or deficit-based? When you think about this observation, what feelings are associated with it?
Think about the student's relationships with peers.		
Think about the student's decision making.		

continues

	What have you observed?	Is this asset- or deficit-based? When you think about this observation, what feelings are associated with it?
Think about the student's relationship with you.		
Think about the student's academic competence.		

Reflect:	**Notes:**
What do you notice about how you described the child? Were the descriptors positive or negative? Deficit- or asset-based? Did you see any patterns in your feelings?	
Synthesize: What do you realize now that you didn't before about your expectations for the child? Are there ways you will look at the student differently moving forward?	

Figure 2.4

Language
That Builds
Relationships

{ difficulty }

Carlos Had a Bad Reputation

In a scene that is all too common in schools, each summer after I received my class list, I frequently heard warnings about certain students from their prior teachers. One warning particularly stands out. That summer as soon as I received my second-grade list, a first-grade teacher started urging me to enjoy my summer as much as possible because my upcoming school year was going to be miserable, thanks to one particular student—Carlos. "The hardest child I ever taught," she insisted, explaining that while Carlos was very capable academically, he was also incredibly defiant, often refusing to comply with even the simplest requests and sometimes shutting down completely. And, she warned, he was very sneaky—taking things from other students, picking on them when she wasn't looking, and quietly causing all sorts of social chaos in her classroom. Every time I saw her, she had a new dire tidbit to share with me.

By the time the school year started, I was very nervous, dreading the first day, dreading this child whom I had not even met. For the first week, I felt as if I were walking on pins and needles and expecting the worst. I know I treated Carlos differently from my other new students and suspect I treated the whole class differently from my prior classes.

After a week or so of this self-inflicted misery, I realized we were all on a disastrous path and made the conscious decision to try to reset my attitude toward Carlos and open my mind to the possibilities a new year might hold. One of the steps I took was reminding myself that among a new group of students, with a new teacher, and with new experiences, Carlos might grow and change. As a result, I made an effort during the second week to get to know him as a person, not just as a reputation. I was quickly and pleasantly surprised at what I discovered. He and I bonded almost immediately over a mutual love of books and football. I also discovered that he was an incredibly talented artist and writer who suffered from near-crippling perfectionism, a condition I was sympathetic to. And he and I developed a particularly playful rapport at recess and lunch, as I discovered his quick, sharp sense of humor. Of course, it took longer than the second week to develop our relationship, but we made a start that week, and, over time, he and I formed quite a bond.

And that bond was necessary to get us through many rough times. As predicted, Carlos was a challenging child to teach. The famed shutdowns happened many times over the course of the year. Once he was so upset that he crawled under a picnic table at the end of recess and refused to budge, forcing me to send for help so that I could take the rest of my class inside and teach. Like his first-grade teacher, I too received complaints from students, and sometimes their families, of secret bullying. Carlos sometimes used his wit to put down his classmates. Moreover, the combination of his moodiness, acerbic wit, and far superior talents in the classroom and on the playing field made his relationships with classmates fraught with difficulty.

Still the year was far, far from miserable. Carlos made so much progress. By the end, he could talk and even laugh about his shutdowns. He had begun to develop some strategies for calming himself down and for verbalizing his feelings. He formed a few friendships, including a surprising one with a very quiet and introverted girl who shared his love of words and art. I also learned a great deal from him that helped me with future students, especially understanding what happens to children's rational brains when they are in a fight-or-flight mode. He still keeps in touch and, last I heard, is doing quite well in life.

The incident with Carlos stands out to me as a reminder of how powerful the language we use in thinking about, discussing, and talking to children can be. That language colors every interaction we have with them. Until I consciously decided to change my internal narrative, I dreaded, feared, and closed my mind to an eight-year-old child. It's very hard for me to admit *that. It affected me physically and emotionally, detracting from my teaching of him and his classmates. Only once I decided to stop listening to my negative internal conversational track did the door open for him and me. It was hard work and didn't lead to some perfect Hollywood ending, but that change in my internal language was essential to moving forward with him.*

And, as I came to realize over years of coaching and teaching, our internal language is inextricably and powerfully linked to our external conversations. When we consistently foster negative thoughts about a child, a group of children, our class as a whole, or teaching itself, those feelings color every word we utter aloud, to our family, friends, colleagues, and students. When we speak out of our internal feelings of fear, negativity, or pessimism, we reinforce our destructive internal conversations, contribute to what can be a toxic school culture, and, of course, damage our relationships with students. To change our language to be more positive and productive, we need to begin with the linchpin, our internal narrative, and then we need to turn to the external—the words we use with colleagues and students.

{ shift }

Change Your Internal Dialogue

We sometimes act as if we have no control over our thoughts, particularly when our feelings are involved. It's as if we say to ourselves, "This is just how I feel; I can't help it." But the truth is that we can control the internal running monologue we have with ourselves.

To get started, it can be helpful to consider the power we have over our thoughts away from the classroom. Think about a time when despite some initial failure, you persevered in learning a new skill or completing a challenging task. Your initial failure might have left you doubtful and internally negative about your abilities. But something within you pushed you to keep trying despite those failures. Think about how you mentally moved yourself to persist despite initial setbacks. What helped? The answer is different for all of us, but it's important to figure out.

For example, I love to cook but for years struggled with successfully making pie crust. My early attempts were so pathetic that for a while I just gave up and purchased the store-bought kind. But, during those store-bought years, I felt this nagging sense that I should be able to do it. I could cook so many other things—why not pie crust? I began to slowly (and secretly because, of course, as a perfectionist, I didn't want anyone to know I had struggled) research the topic, reading everything I could about the science of this delicate pastry. Then I met my future mother-in-law, who patiently gave me some lessons and shared her own recipe. I didn't have instant success, but I just kept telling myself I could do it. I didn't let my failures get in the way, and I also had enough glimpses of success along the way to keep me going. And perhaps most importantly, I can now make a pretty mean pie crust.

Unfortunately, there is no magic quick fix to reset our narratives. It requires consistent, concentrated effort, frequently catching ourselves in the moment of negativity. With that effort, our narratives will change over time, maybe not completely, but for the better. From working on my own internal conversations and helping many teachers do the same with theirs, I have discovered that actions like the following can help.

{ strategy }

Switch to
Growth-Oriented Language

As with my pie-crust endeavors, I frequently had to remind myself that change with a particular student was possible. That meant moving from a "can't/impossible" mind-set to a "can/possible" one. Switching mind-sets can be challenging and might first require some grounding, such as

- acknowledging, without blame, your negative feelings;

- breathing deeply;

- engaging in some quick movement or exercise; and

- playing music or watching a lighthearted video to get yourself in a more positive frame of mind.

Once you have prepared yourself to take on the challenge of changing your mind-set, it can be helpful to do an exercise like the one in Figure 3.1. Describe as concretely as possible the challenges you're facing with a child, consider how those challenges have led to a deficit mind-set about the child, and develop more positive, appreciative language about the child and your relationship with him or her. Then see Figure 3.2 for some additional ways to work on switching your language with students.

Behaviors the Child Exhibits	Deficit, Fixed Language About the Relationship	Appreciative, Growth Language About the Relationship
	SWITCH TO GROWTH-ORIENTED LANGUAGE	
• Seems bored or inattentive during instructional times • Rarely does work at independent work times	"She is just like her brother. He never paid attention, and his mom didn't care. It's hopeless. I'll just have to muddle through with her, just like I did with him."	"I never formed a strong relationship with her brother, but that doesn't mean I can't have one with her. I am going to start by trying to get to know her better. I am going to remember to take this one day at a time."
• Makes mean comments to friends • Has trouble taking turns during partner or group work • Refuses to share materials during partner and group work	"This child is impossible. He is ruining everything for my class and me."	"This child is harder than many children I have taught, and I feel protective of other kids when he is mean. But he is not my enemy. I can get to know him just like I have gotten to know so many children before him. I can find positives about him."

continues

Behaviors the Child Exhibits	Deficit, Fixed Language About the Relationship	Appreciative, Growth Language About the Relationship
• Frequently questions teacher's authority • Often refuses to follow even the simplest directions • Gets angry quickly and lashes out at the teacher and her peers	"What can I possibly do with a kid like this? I have tried being nice, but she's not trying. Every time I try to help her, she rejects me."	"What I've tried so far hasn't worked, but I am going to hold onto my belief that every child has potential. I think I need to get some help from my colleagues. I know that with help, my relationship with this child can get better."

Figure 3.1

{commitment}

Plan Asset-Based Language

To develop your skill with switching your language to a more growth-oriented mind-set, choose one child with whom you're struggling. Acknowledge that you're stuck, and describe what you are seeing with the child. Then, under "Deficit, Fixed Language About the Relationship," write out the language you're using that keeps you stuck: "This child can't . . . ," "I can't . . . ," and so on. Then try to move past the "can't" statements by reframing your thinking more positively. To help you, consider the following questions:

- What words do I need to remove from my thinking (e.g., *never, impossible, every time*)?
- How can I focus on the relationship without the child's other challenges getting in the way?
- What strengths do I have that can foster my relationship with the child?
- Can I reframe some of the child's challenges as strengths that might help in our relationship?

Deficit, Fixed Language About the Relationship	Appreciative, Growth Language About the Relationship

Figure 3.2

Return to your new language model often as you work with the child, or redo this exercise if you find yourself slipping into previous negative patterns.

Develop Compassionate Curiosity

As we explain in Section 1, intentionally working on developing compassion for a child improves the relationship. Compassion does not mean feeling pity for the child. Rather it involves moving beyond personalizing the difficulty as about us and centering our attention on who the child is and what the child needs. For me, it helps to either mentally or, in more challenging cases, physically remind myself. One year my bathroom mirror was covered with sticky notes that said things like this:

- → If he were my child, how would I want him treated?

- → If this were my niece or nephew, what would I want his or her teacher to do?

- → This child is only eleven years old. How can I write her off?

- → The child's behavior has nothing to do with you. See past it.

- → What more is there to know about this child, beyond the difficulty we're having?

With Carlos, my realization that I hadn't really give him a chance forced me to intentionally set out to find out more about his likes, dislikes, and interests. My relationship with him was able to flourish only once I committed to compassionate curiosity. See Figure 3.3 for ways to reframe your thinking.

{commitment}

Reframe Your Thinking

Choose a child with whom you are struggling. Try out the exercise, and consider how you can move toward compassionate curiosity.

This child is only _____ years old. The child can be his or her best self only if the child knows adults care about him or her.

Three Things I Admire About This Child:

_____

_____

_____

Three Things This Child Loves:

_____

_____

_____

Figure 3.3

Change Your Mind-Set
Through Positive Actions

Often we can reset a negative internal narrative by considering and taking concrete positive actions. Sometimes just the act of doing something positive can make us feel more optimistic. Accordingly, I often tried to list specific things I could do to help a troubling situation. One year in my planner I listed these steps to take with a challenging student:

➤ Give Jayden at least two specific pieces of positive feedback.

➤ Remember to start with a clean slate.

➤ Write a reinforcing note and slip it into his homework folder.

➤ Check in with Jayden about how he liked the new Star Wars movie.

➤ Find out how Jayden is feeling about *Wonder*. Explore other books he might like.

Forcing ourselves to do something can jolt us out of our negativity. With Carlos, trying to remember to start each day with a clean slate and making sure I pointed out one positive thing helped both of us feel more optimistic each day. See Figure 3.4 for additional suggestions.

{commitment}

Brainstrom Positive Actions

Think of a child or children with whom you are struggling. List some positive actions you could take to reset your mind-set.

Child	Action

Figure 3.4

{ **strategy** }

Practice Mindful Attention

Many teachers I have worked with have found that engaging in mindfulness practices, even for a few minutes a day, could help them reset their thinking about a particular student and put their overall experiences in a better perspective. They also reported that these techniques could help them get through moments of stress they encountered with students.

Here are some mindfulness techniques you can try:

_____ ***Learn breathing exercises.*** Try this simple one to start: Count from fifty to one backward, coordinating your counting with breaths in and out. At fifty, breathe in; at forty-nine, breathe out; and so on. Or count from twenty-five down to one. Pay attention to how you feel before and after this technique.

_____ ***Practice guided meditation.*** Try apps like Headspace or 10% Happier, which have some free material or a free trial period. Or go to YouTube and search for "guided meditation" and try some free videos by respected practitioners like Joseph Goldstein, Kristin Neff, Angel Kyodo Williams, and Shinzen Young. Find a personality who works well for you.

_____ ***Practice being in the moment*** by using your senses more. Stop at certain times of the day and notice the sights, smells, sounds, and textures around you. What do you see, feel, hear?

For more ideas, see *Happy Teachers Change the World*, by Hanh and Weare (2017).

None of these practices results in immediate calm or perfection, but stick with them and you (and others) will notice a change in your internal stance. Choose one to try, and stick with it at least for several weeks; new research says it takes sixty-six days to change or incorporate a behavior (Lally et al. 2009). Note the difference it makes in your internal and external conversations.

{ strategy }

Attend to Your Life Beyond School

Although it sounds trite, in order to foster more positive internal language toward students, we have to make sure that we are taking care of our own physical, social, and emotional needs. Teaching is so personal and hard—it takes a lot out of us physically and emotionally. There's always more we can do to improve our instruction and relationships with children; it is easy to put our own needs aside. But if we don't take time for ourselves, we cannot do our best for students. To have the energy to take on this challenging work, we need to exercise, be cared for and care for others outside of school, and have passions and interests other than our students.

Ways to Care for Your Own Needs

_____ Exercise.

_____ Have conversations about something other than work.

_____ Read a book for fun or pick up a magazine that you've never read before.

_____ Go out with friends.

_____ Do volunteer work.

_____ Take a class that is not about teaching.

_____ Call a friend you haven't talked to in a while.

_____ Cultivate a new hobby.

For more ideas, see _The Well-Balanced Teacher_, by Mike Anderson (2010).

If you're not already doing some of these things, choose one or two. Make a plan for how you can stick with them. Work with a colleague to hold each other to your commitments.

Teachers who make the time to take care of their own physical and emotional needs find a renewed energy and strength to think proactively about challenging school situations. They can be more creative about and open to possible next steps with students. They also feel more positive overall so that when some of their proactive steps fail, which inevitably happens, they can simply regroup rather than feel like a failure, blame the child, or give up.

{ shift }

Change Your Public Conversations

Although resetting our internal narratives about children is an essential first step, we can't stop there. We also need to change what comes out of our mouths, beginning with our public conversations about children with whom we struggle. The way we talk about them with colleagues especially can reinforce our negativity toward them, our indifference to them, or our sense of hopelessness. Instead we can talk to colleagues in a way that is productive, can challenge us to move beyond that first primal brain response that we talked about in the introduction, and can help us to use our rational brains to implement helpful strategies and interventions. Becoming aware of ineffective or damaging language and changing our language habits can go a long way to helping us succeed with children who challenge us.

A good starting place for developing our awareness is to reflect on why it is so easy for conversations about children, especially challenging ones, to go negative. Often, we unconsciously offer harsh criticism of and negativity toward a child we are teaching to relieve the guilt and failure we feel about working with them. It's as if we're saying, "It's not my fault. This child is impossible."

And when we share these thoughts with our colleagues, they often respond just as negatively because they are sympathetic, they've been there themselves, and they want to make us feel better. They want to alleviate our obvious burden, and they do that by not so subtly reinforcing the idea that all of the struggles we are experiencing are because the child is flawed, not because of what we have done or could do—there is nothing we can do about the situation!

Often these impulses can lead to very unhealthy dynamics with our colleagues. After discovering that if we complain about a child, we'll receive sympathy and reassurance that it's the child, not us, we complain more often. Our colleagues reciprocate with their tales of challenging and impossible students, and we respond with sympathy toward them. It doesn't take long for a teaching community to establish extremely negative communication patterns.

In some ways, it is very similar to the way many people in our country have built bubbles in which we communicate about politics and other contentious issues only with those who we know will lend a sympathetic ear and reinforce our own views. When we disparage a particular leader or party to those in our circle, they jump right in and tell us how right we are. They might even add more reasons to support our claims.

But, in the same way that talking only to people who agree with us politically can prevent us from considering different ideas and receiving potentially helpful information, the cycle of negative conversations about children can often shut down our divergent thinking and discourage us from considering other options for what to do. These negative conversations also reinforce the biases we bring to our work. And while it might bring temporary relief to hear that it's the child, not us, it does absolutely nothing to help us do anything about the challenges we face.

Talk More to Explore Solutions

So what should we do? We can't just stop talking to colleagues. Teaching can be so isolating. We actually need to talk more, not less. And with their knowledge and experience, our fellow teachers often have a great deal to offer us in the way of new ideas and approaches. We need to find productive ways to harness their knowledge and experience and to relieve some of our own sense of failure and isolation.

One way to do this is to be more intentional about which colleagues we talk to and how these conversations look. Both in my teaching and in my consulting life, I have found it incredibly powerful to stop discussing challenging students with colleagues who I know are ready and willing to put these children down. I still have relationships with those colleagues, but we just talk about other things. If they bring up their own challenges, I am genuinely empathetic—"I know how hard that is" or "Oh, you must feel so frustrated"—but I refrain from taking that next step into insulting the child or the child's family.

At each school where I have worked, I developed a small cadre of colleagues with whom I could have serious conversations about students with whom I was struggling. I found my way to people who I knew would be empathetic but who would also stay positive and help me take effective action. I found people who I knew would help me think about what to do and, when appropriate, challenge my negativity or try to help me move past my initial fatalistic views.

Depending upon what your faculty culture is like, making the transition from toxic conversations to more productive ones can be challenging. It can affect your own sense of belonging to feel as if you're no longer going to be one of the team who are happy to join in with blaming children. But I have also found at every school where I worked that many people are secretly relieved to find an escape from those conversations. I have always been able to find a group of colleagues who provided each other support around challenging children without putting those children down.

I also have found it helpful to clearly express what I want from conversations with colleagues. There have been times when I have said, "I just need to vent. Please don't feel like you need to say anything. It would just be helpful for you to listen." At other times, I might say that I'm feeling frustrated and explain what happened but then let my colleague know that I'd love some honest feedback about what he or she thinks I could do differently.

Here's how these strategies played out with those colleagues who gave me summer warnings about future students. First, I tried to keep my conversations with them centered on social topics, not students. And if they did try to initiate their warnings, I tried to redirect them through questions: "Did you find positives or strengths in this child?" or "She does sound challenging. What strategies did you try?" I found that even the most negative colleague could often come up with a positive point or at least share some helpful advice. With one colleague, I even found the inner courage to speak up, saying, "I know that you are trying to help me, but when you tell me how terrible my year is going to be because of a certain child, it doesn't help and just stresses me out. I'd love to get your insights about children but in a way that feels more hopeful for the children and me." And to her credit, she listened and really tried. Over time, our conversations about children improved.

Use a Conversation Protocol

Another way to promote productive discussions is to engage in more formal conversations about children with colleagues. In these conversations, one teacher follows a specific protocol for presenting a challenge to a small group of colleagues, who in turn offer questions and suggestions for interventions. Following a specific protocol for such conversations can help shed new light on a situation and maximize the input of colleagues. At the end of a half-hour gripe session, we often have nothing more to show than a strong sense of outrage at a student, but after spending the same amount of time following a structured protocol, we can leave with a whole list of new ideas and strategies to try.

Such structured conversations work best when everyone involved has built a strong level of trust and has a shared understanding of the participants' goals for working with students. Trust is essential, as the person presenting the challenge has to feel confident that her colleagues won't judge or gossip about her and her teaching afterward. This shared understanding helps the teacher have confidence that her colleagues' suggestions will be ones she actually might be comfortable trying out. There is no magic number for the size of these groups, but I have found that they work best when there are at least five people involved.

There are many protocols available to guide these conversations. The one I have found easiest and most productive to use is simple, involving the following five steps, adapted from *Responsive School Discipline: Essentials for Elementary School Leaders* (Wood and Freeman-Loftis 2011):

1. Introduction

2. Problem

3. Clarification

4. Suggestions

5. Closing

It is important that all participants understand how each step works and the thinking behind each:

1. **Introduction:** Review the ground rules and procedure. At its first meeting, the group should adopt ground rules that at a minimum address the following:

   ➤ having respect for the teacher presenting the problem and the child(ren) about whom the teacher is presenting

   ➤ ensuring confidentiality so that the teacher knows that others will not discuss the challenge with anyone who is not at the meeting and will honor the child's right to privacy

   ➤ agreeing that no one will follow up with the presenting teacher unless he or she asks for more input or revisits topics from the protocol conversation, so that the presenting teacher does not feel obligated to discuss the situation again unless he or she wants to (Such a ground rule maintains a teacher's sense of efficacy, keeping the teacher from that feeling of being monitored and judged that is so ever-present in our schools.)

   Also, the group should decide during this step whether the presenting teacher or one of the other participants will take notes.

2. **Problem:** One teacher presents the challenging situation in specific, descriptive detail. This step can require that we develop new skills, as many of us are most used to describing situations in generalities ("He is annoying," "She is lazy," "He doesn't even try to do his work") and absolutes ("She never says anything nice," "He always interrupts me"). However, labels and general descriptions will not help the listeners get a vivid picture of what is happening and what might help. The teacher describing the problem needs to be as specific as possible, describing exactly what a child has done or said in several concrete situations.

3. **Clarification:** Others ask clarifying questions, and the teacher responds. These questions should not jump ahead to the next step by being suggestions in disguise. Instead the questions should help all listeners better understand the child and the challenges the child and teacher face.

4. **Suggestions:** Others suggest possible interventions or next steps. The teacher listens without comment or judgment. The goal is for the teacher who presented the challenge to listen as openly as possible and try to imagine new possibilities for his or her work with the child. Having the teacher remain silent during the presentation of ideas encourages him or her to try to take in the suggestions without judgment or defense. Instead of replying, "I already tried that," or "I don't think that will work," the teacher or whoever is taking notes just keeps all of the ideas as possibilities. Obviously, the teacher can discard them later if he or she has already tried them. But in many cases, I and teachers I have known have reconsidered strategies that we have already tried or dismissed once we've heard others suggest them. We might realize, for example, that we didn't give an idea enough time to work when we initially tried it or that we didn't enter into the intervention with the same spirit we might be able to deploy now. Silent listening and reflection help foster this openness to new possibility.

   When the conversation involves a behavior challenge, it can be helpful to divide this step into two subparts: (1) suggestions for proactive steps that the teacher can consider taking to set the child up for success with a particular behavior, and (2) responsive steps that the teacher can consider taking when the child has behavior challenges.

5. **Closing:** Everyone reflects on the process. During this step the teacher does not respond to the suggestions. If he or she chooses, the teacher might follow up with one of the group members later

to find out more about an idea that person shared, but at this point in the protocol, it often works best simply to have the teacher sit with some of the ideas and let them percolate. The teacher merely thanks the group members for their time and effort.

It can then be helpful for group members to rename the goals of confidentiality and following up only if the presenting teacher requests further assistance. Sometimes groups find it beneficial also to reflect on what went well process-wise, not in terms of the actual content of the meeting, and to adjust ground rules as needed.

To flesh out how the protocol works, I share an example of how it looked when I was the presenting teacher. I met with several colleagues I trusted: a few classroom teachers, one special area teacher, and one of my administrators. We did not have a school counselor, but that person can often offer invaluable insights during these discussions.

Conversation Protocol in Action

1. *Introduction* (five minutes): My colleagues and I adhered to the following guidelines for our discussions:

    ➡ Speak about the child's actions, not his or her character.

    ➡ Presume positive intentions.

    ➡ Keep it confidential.

    ➡ Leave the discussion at the meeting.

    To honor everyone's time, we also agreed to and respected certain time limits for the conversation. I've added these to the steps in parentheses. Someone agreed to be the timekeeper. I preferred to take my own notes in these conversations and would tell my colleagues that during this step.

2. *Problem* (five minutes): I presented the case of a second grader who frequently became incredibly upset at seemingly small setbacks. I shared the following specifics:

    ➡ Several times the child has come back from PE red in the face and in tears. When I ask what is wrong, he snaps, "Leave me alone," or physically lashes out at me. For example, on one occasion, he pushed his desk over at me after I tried to figure out what had happened during PE. On that occasion when I asked the PE teacher for more information, the teacher had no idea what had happened to upset the student.

➜ On several other occasions, the child has had trouble completing an academic assignment. Writing seems especially hard. During several writing assignments, the child has wadded up his paper and thrown it on the floor, burst into tears, and slammed his head down on his notebook.

➜ Many episodes occur outside of class, such as in PE or at lunch or recess.

➜ After the child gets upset, it takes him a considerably long time, sometimes until the end of the school day, to regain his composure.

➜ I have tried to talk with the child about what is going on, but he has had a very hard time telling me what is wrong or how I can help. His parents have offered some clues, explaining that he thinks other students are bullying him and that he doesn't feel like he fits in at school.

3. *Clarification* (five minutes): As usual, my colleagues asked some very insightful questions. I have included these and my responses to them:

Q: Does he appear to become more upset later in the day than earlier?

A: Yes, now that I think about it, he does have a harder time as the day goes on.

Q: What does he enjoy about school, and what are his strengths?

A: He enjoys reading and math, especially. He is also very artistic and loves to draw and build. He loves it when I read aloud and loves our class meetings.

Q: Does he have any friends?

A: He is friendly with many children but does not yet have close friends.

Q: What is he like when he is not upset? How is his relationship with you?

A: When he is not upset, he is very sweet. He has a great sense of humor and is very curious, especially about history and art. We laugh and joke, and I know both from him and from his parents that he is really enjoying many aspects of school despite his struggles.

4. *Suggestions* (fifteen minutes): Here are some strategies my colleagues suggested:

➔ Have someone go watch what happens in PE for several days. The colleague suggesting this felt that it would be helpful for someone else to observe because (1) my presence might affect how my students behaved and (2) I needed to have a break from the unease caused by the frequent but unexpected explosions from the child.

➔ Teach the child some self-soothing strategies, getting help from experts as needed.

➔ For one week, take consistent and detailed notes about what happens during each scheduled block (writing, math, etc.) of the day.

➔ Build in times for a break for the student, for example, having an administrator or a special area teacher take him for a walk. Teach the child to recognize when a break would be helpful.

➔ Consider what kind of academic supports the child might need. In particular, consider using scaffolds to make writing more successful and enjoyable.

➔ Spend some one-on-one time with the child without discussing any problems.

→ Find ways to give the child added nonstressful responsibilities, such as helping in a younger class or helping to draw or build something for a classroom display.

→ Develop an emergency plan for when the child is very upset so that I will feel more comfortable letting him calm down on his own while keeping those around him safe.

→ Share more frequently about what is happening with one or more people in the group instead of trying to handle it all on my own.

→ Have a trusted colleague or administrator observe the class to see if he or she notices any bullying or other problems with friends.

5. **Closing** (five minutes): I thanked my colleagues for their help. Indeed, I remember feeling heartened for the first time in a long time about this situation. We talked about how hard it is not to follow up, as it's human to want to make sure the colleague is feeling OK, but we also reminded ourselves why this step was important. Figure 3.5 provides a tool to plan for these conversations.

Conversation Protocol Worksheet

1. Introduction

Whom do you want to invite to the conversation? _____

_____

What ground rules would be helpful?_____

_____

Would you rather take notes or have someone do it for you? _____

_____

2. Problem

How can you concretely but succinctly describe what is happening?
What specifics can you offer? _____

_____

3. Clarification _____

_____

_____

4. Suggestions

What strategies will you use to keep an open mind and fully listen to
colleagues' suggestions? _____

_____

5. Closing

_____

_____

Figure 3.5

{shift}

Change How You Speak to Children

The third aspect of language we must attend to is how we speak with children. The way we speak to our students has a tremendous impact on our relationship with them, their view of themselves, and their classmates' relationship with them. Haim Ginott's famous quote always helps me remember the power of the language we use with students:

> I've come to a frightening conclusion that I am the decisive element in the classroom. It's my personal approach that creates the climate. It's my daily mood that makes the weather. As a teacher, I possess a tremendous power to make a child's life miserable or joyous. I can be a tool of torture or an instrument of inspiration. I can humiliate or heal. In all situations, it is my response that decides whether a crisis will be escalated or de-escalated and a child humanized or dehumanized. (1972, 15–16)

It can be hard to accept or shoulder this responsibility, but it exists. The words we say and the way we say them have powerful and lasting effects. We need to be mindful both of key practices with language and how to approach changing the language we use with students. We also need to admit when the language we use is counterproductive. Of course, our language doesn't cause students' problems, but it can certainly exacerbate them.

Imagine a child who frequently says unkind things to others and often has trouble cooperating in games or work situations. You watch as another student tells that student she can't join in a game they are playing at indoor recess. Of course, nothing you said caused this situation to happen, but what you say after it happens can greatly affect the child and her classmates, as shown in Figure 3.6.

EXAMINING THE EFFECTS OF LANGUAGE

You Say	Impact
"Well, what do you expect? You are never nice to them, so your classmates don't want to play with you."	• The child feels resentment toward you and the other children. • The child feels worse about herself. • She feels as if she does not belong. • She may act out more to show that she doesn't care.

Compare the above response to this:

You Say	Impact
[To the children who are excluding] "That was unkind. Our rules say we will include others." **[To the child who is excluded]** "That must have hurt your feelings. If you would still like to join them, I will sit with all of you to help the game go smoothly."	• The child knows her feelings matter. • The child realizes the rules apply to everyone. • The child might think that, with help, she can learn to play with others.

Figure 3.6

Ginott and other authors have written comprehensive guidance on how to communicate with students in caring and productive ways (see, e.g., Paula Denton's *The Power of Our Words* [2015] and Peter H. Johnston's *Choice Words* [2004] and *Opening Minds: Using Language to Change Lives* [2012]). For the purposes of this book, I want to highlight just a few key strategies that are particularly essential in supporting students with whom we don't yet have positive relationships.

{ strategy }

Use a Genuine Tone

Often as a coach or an administrator, I could tell almost immediately how a teacher felt about a student just from the tone of voice she used, even if she was saying something positive to a child. In these instances of positive feedback, that tone sounded false, sometimes singsong or oddly upbeat, and different from the tone the teacher used with other students. Even more problematic, when teachers were upset with these students, both their tone and the words themselves often were harsh, judgmental, and closed off. Again, they spoke in a very different way from how they spoke to students with whom they had more positive relationships.

In many ways this difference in tone was understandable because these teachers had not formed a strong relationship with these students. We speak differently with people with whom we are close. But it's critical to be aware of the differences and try as much as possible to use a more genuine and authentic tone. And if you notice yourself using a false tone, recognize that as an indicator that you need to put time into your relationship with that student. Children can hear and feel the difference, and it can exacerbate their sense of isolation from their teacher and classmates when their teacher doesn't sound the same when communicating with them as with others.

To work on your tone, consider the following points:

➜ Be aware of your physical state and reactions. If your throat is tight or you are clenching muscles somewhere in your body, it will be hard to speak in a genuine, relaxed tone. Pause, take a deep breath, relax your muscles, and try again.

➜ Pay attention to how you speak to a student with whom you have a great relationship and try to adopt that tone with all students.

➜ Practice using a more even tone in advance of your work with the student.

➜ Adjust your tone in the moment when you hear yourself sounding overly harsh or patronizingly positive.

{ strategy }

Address Actions, Not Character

Both when pointing out positives and redirecting a student who has made mistakes, whether academically or behaviorally, focus on what the student has done, instead of making generalizations about what kind of person the student is or what attributes she has. Consider the differences in the examples shown in Figure 3.7.

**GENERAL OR CHARACTER-BASED LANGUAGE
VERSUS SPECIFIC LANGUAGE**

Situation	Problematic Generalities or Character-Focused Language	Beneficial Specific Language
A child who often struggles to get along with peers has a successful interaction.	"You did such an awesome job in that math game. What a good sport you can be!"	*[Privately]* "Cassie and you got along well during that math game. You took turns, you followed the rules, you complimented her, and you kept your cool when you lost. It looks like you had fun and learned more about multiplication."

continues

Situation	Problematic Generalities or Character-Focused Language	Beneficial Specific Language
A child who has trouble keeping his personal and school materials neat and organized drops everything out of his desk during math class.	"Again? You are such a mess. I don't know how you ever find anything in there. Looks like you'll be missing recess to clean up."	*[Privately]* "Move your things aside for now so you can keep focusing on math. When you are finished, you can use our desk-organizing chart to clean up. Let me know if you need more help."
A child who struggles with controlling her temper and ordinarily would have sworn at someone who got in her personal space says nothing when a classmate accidentally trips and runs into her desk.	"Wow, you didn't blow up like you usually do at Demetrius. I am super impressed that you didn't cuss. I wasn't sure you had it in you."	*[Privately]* "You showed a lot of self-control when Demetrius ran into your desk. And I saw you ask him if he was OK. You really took him being in your space in stride."

Figure 3.7

Focusing on students' actions, rather than their alleged characters, forces you to be more neutral and educative in your feedback to students. They in turn receive concrete information upon which they can build. If it is information about something they did well, they can use that information to try to repeat their success. If it is about a mistake, they can use that information to try to correct it or avoid it in the future. There is, in contrast, little they can do when someone asserts that they are lazy or careless. Also, comments about character often lead to a defensive response—such remarks feel more like a personal attack than a teachable moment. Use Figure 3.8 to practice shifting your language.

{commitment}

Replace Problematic Language

To work on your own use of language, record, have a colleague record, or just think of how you speak to students and write out some common phrases. Take phrases or comments in which you are addressing a child's character, not her actions, and do a rewrite.

Situation	Problematic Generalities or Character-Focused Language	Beneficial Specific Language

© 2019 by Gianna Cassetta and Margaret Wilson from *The Caring Teacher*. Portsmouth, NH: Heinemann.

Figure 3.8

The more you practice action-oriented language, especially if you practice such language ahead of time, the more likely you will be to internalize this language and have it ready to use when you need it.

Speak Directly and Privately to Students

When you have something to say about a student, say it to that student, not the class or group in which the student is working, and whenever possible, strive to do so privately. Sometimes in an effort to avoid confrontation, teachers make general statements to the whole class about one or a few students, such as "I'm noticing some people are forgetting to turn in their homework," or "I've heard some people insult their partners' reading during paired reading." But these indirect statements are problematic. First, often the very students whose actions we want to influence fail to realize that we are talking about them through these statements. However, their classmates often immediately know whom we're talking about and feel emboldened by these public put-downs to make fun of the students in question or at least to feel superior to them. Relationships suffer as a result. Children who already struggle can easily fall into a "the whole world is against me" mind-set. Moreover, any time we speak indirectly we undermine our trust with students, as they learn there are often hidden meanings and undercurrents to our words.

Privacy is also especially important, particularly with students with whom we have not yet developed a strong relationship. Public redirection or correction can make students feel unsafe and ridiculed and can lead some students to publicly confront us in return. Frequent public redirection, especially if accompanied by put-downs or generalities, can diminish a student's standing in the eyes of classmates, exacerbating preexisting social challenges the student might have faced. When we put students down, their classmates might feel entitled to do the same and might even do so to let us know they agree with us, creating a negative cycle of interaction for already troubled students. Public praise is less problematic, but it can still make many students feel uncomfortable and can foster unproductive feelings of competitiveness among students, as some may think, "I did the same thing. Why isn't she praising me?"

{ strategy }

Match Language to Intent

One of the hardest things to recognize about the language we use with children is that while we have one message in mind, the words we use convey all sorts of different, and sometimes damaging, unintended messages. For example, knowing that to learn, students need to be productive and on-task during independent work times, I often tried to use words to get them back on track when they appeared to be staring off into space, goofing off, or otherwise not engaged in the task at hand. Like many teachers, I was often multitasking, usually working with another student or a small group. I hated to interrupt that work, so I would just speak to the unproductive child from where I was. Often, it was brief and direct: "Andrew, get back to work!" Although I said it respectfully, I was unconsciously giving these messages as well:

- → The task at hand is drudgery ("work").

- → The reason to do the drudgery is because I say so (i.e., not because of the learning you will do).

- → I am the boss around here, and it is my job to make sure you get the drudgery done.

Of course, none of those reflects what I really believe or even what I meant in the moment.

To be more intentional with our words is hard. And if we overly examine each of the thousand sentences we say every day, we could drive ourselves crazy. But neither of those facts negates the need to be more intentional with language and the benefits of doing so. Over time we can slowly change our behaviors and words to more closely align with what we mean and believe.

For example, as I grew in my confidence as a teacher, I learned that unless a child was being disruptive, it was OK for me to notice her not writing during writing time or solving math problems during math time and not respond immediately. I could finish up with the student or small group I was working with or get them to a point of some independence and then go check in with the child who appeared not to be working. At that point, I could be more intentional about my language. Often I would just ask, "How is it going?" I was shocked to discover how much this simple question could help me unpack. At writing times, this question and the answers that followed helped me realize that just like I do, children often need to think when they write and a child might have been doing just that. And across subject areas, I came to see that what often led children not to be "working" wasn't going to be fixed by me ordering them to do so. Often bigger problems were in play.

Taking the time to make sure we are being precise in our language and conveying what we mean is well worth it. Often, the shifts we make can be simple but powerful. Here are a few examples in Figure 3.9:

UNDERSTANDING OUR MESSAGES			
What We Sometimes Say	**What the Message Is**	**More Intentional Replacement Language**	**What the Message Is**
"It makes me so happy when you all are kind to each other."	The reason to be kind is to make me happy.	"It seems like everyone had a much better recess because you were kind to each other. What a great day for our community!"	The reason to be kind is that it helps everyone in our community.
"If you get this work done, we'll have extra time for recess."	Academic work is hard and unrewarding; recess is fun.	"It's going to be very exciting to see and hear the writing everyone has done. Let's strive for everyone to have something to share in ten minutes."	Academic work is joyful, purposeful, and productive.

continues

UNDERSTANDING OUR MESSAGES *continued*			
What We Sometimes Say	**What the Message Is**	**More Intentional Replacement Language**	**What the Message Is**
"How many times do I have to explain these directions?"	I think there is something wrong with you because I have explained what to do so many times, and you still don't get it or won't do it.	"I've posted the directions on the board. Check with a friend if you have trouble understanding them."	I trust you to read the directions and figure out what to do.

Figure 3.9

As the last example in Figure 3.10 demonstrates, one particularly tricky aspect of using language more intentionally is our use of questions. Unfortunately, we often ask questions to which we don't really want answers or that don't even have answers. For example, when children have made mistakes, we might ask, "Why did you do that?" or "Why can't you just _____?" Students really have no answers to these questions, and the questions don't lead to any improvements in behavior. A good rule of thumb in all interactions with students is to only ask questions that are meaningful and will lead students to think productively about their actions.

{commitment}
Use Intentional Language

To help develop your understanding of the impact of language and your skill at being more intentional, consider some of these common teacher statements, analyze what the message is, write replacement language, and then analyze its message.

What We Sometimes Say	What the Message Is	More Intentional Replacement Language	What the Message Is
"It makes me so sad when my friends [the students] don't use their time wisely and then have to miss recess."			
"You get what you get and you don't pitch a fit."			
"Why did you do that? What were you thinking?"			

Figure 3.10

   As with our internal conversations and the discussions we have with colleagues, we can change the language we use with students first by making a conscious commitment about what to change and why. Then we need to take concrete actions to bring that change about, for example, by drafting language we might use in specific moments or catching our mistakes and revising them midsentence.

section

04

Relatedness

{ difficulty }

Charlotte Felt Out of Sync

I once taught a student who could best be described as out of sync. Charlotte had a hard time with all aspects of school life. She was physically awkward, often bumping into other people, struggling with organizing or transporting her things (which, as a result, were everywhere), and exhibiting extreme sensitivity to loud noises or the feel of certain substances, like the soil we were studying in science. Socially she struggled to connect with her classmates. She had a quirky sense of humor that they often did not understand, and she had a habit of correcting them or telling on them, even for minor problems. I also struggled in my relationship with her, as she frequently pointed out my errors, and most of our contact involved her reports of other students' flaws. She had few real visible areas of interest, so for both her classmates and me, it was hard to get a conversation started or to maintain one. Charlotte also struggled academically, but in puzzling ways. She often seemed to have the basic skills mastered for a particular subject area but couldn't put those together in a meaningful way, and although she could often articulate what she should do on a particular assignment, she often couldn't actually do it.

As with many of the children we discuss in this book, Charlotte had many needs and issues to address, which could feel overwhelming. I knew that there were many issues for which her family and I would need to consult outside experts and resources. However, I also recognized that there were actions I could take that would help. I could exert a great deal of influence over how I treated her, how her classmates treated her, and how she felt about herself. By taking these crucial actions, I could help her at least partially meet those basic emotional needs we outlined earlier—the needs to feel related and competent and to have some autonomy. In this section, I focus on the first need: strategies for helping Charlotte and other students feel a sense of relatedness at school.

To help students feel a stronger sense of connection to others at school, we need to foster their relationships with us and with their fellow students. Building a strong sense of community makes it more likely that students whose classmates might previously have written them off as insignificant, annoying, or unlikable will begin to be more fully integrated into the community. It also increases the chance that students who do not struggle as much will learn to look out for those who do. And perhaps just as importantly, having closer connections with all of our students helps our work feel more purposeful and joyful.

Working to help Charlotte feel more connected to her classmates and me did not solve every problem she had, but this work did have big payoffs for her and us socially and academically. She began to relax more at school so she worried less and less about mistakes her classmates and I were making. As her reports of minor infractions decreased, we in turn felt more relaxed around her, not waiting tensely for her to point out our next mistake. Her increasing ease also helped Charlotte persevere on challenging assignments and be more open to asking for my help with them. Her classmates and I too began to see strengths and interests revealed through our various activities and classroom discussions. We discovered she was a talented artist and passionate cat lover, and we began to understand and appreciate her sense of humor. Once we discovered her immense love of cats, children started to recommend books and movies to her; she visibly brightened as her classmates often gave her a quick smile or glance whenever a read-aloud referred to cats or when we saw a picture of one in a piece of artwork. She was able to leverage this interest academically as she researched how ancient Egyptians valued and cared for cats, even into the afterlife.

{ shift }

Intentionally and Continuously Foster Classroom Community

Our work with individual students begins with our work with the class as a whole. All students need a chance to get to know everyone, not just the people they might already happen to know. They also need to learn how to be part of a trusting and productive classroom community. Such intentional work gives every student at least a fighting chance to fit in and feel connected, and it gives us a foundation on which to build when we need to work with students individually on their social skills and ability to connect with others. Consider some of these steps:

➤ Include intensive community-building work at the beginning of the school year.

➤ Intentionally teach community expectations.

➤ Use class rules as an anchor all year.

➤ Engage in daily community meetings.

➤ Foster inclusion and collaboration.

➤ Use challenging social situations as teachable moments.

➤ Pair and group students in varied ways.

➤ Notice when students are absent.

As you read more about each of these steps, consider your current practice, what you might want to change, and what ideas you might want to add.

{ strategy }

Build Community
Right from the Start

The first few weeks of school are critical to helping students and us get off on the right foot together. Devote time during those weeks to activities and academic lessons that give students a chance to learn more about each other. Figures 4.1–4.4 are a few of our favorite ones, which are simple and flexible, capable of being used multiple times and in different ways.

COMMUNITY-BUILDING ACTIVITIES	
Activity	**Description**
Student survey	Students complete a survey or create a display area to share key facts about themselves, their hobbies, and their interests. (See example on page 92.)
Venn diagram	Students work in pairs to complete a Venn diagram about their similarities and differences. (See example on page 93.)
Two-circle discussion	1. With teacher guidance, students form two concentric circles. 2. Students in the inner circle turn to face those in the outer circle. 3. The teacher then poses a question, such as • "What is one of your favorite books and why?" • "What was something you especially enjoyed about school last year and why?" • "What is your favorite subject at school and why?"

continues

Two-circle discussion *(continued)*	4. After discussing the question with one partner, on the teacher's signal, students in the inner circle move to the next partner in the outer circle and begin again. 5. Students share out key facts they learned about others.
Three-question interview	1. Students draft three open-ended questions they could ask to get to know a classmate. 2. Over several days, students meet with various other assigned classmates, asking their questions and answering those of their partners. 3. Students share out what they've learned. (See example on page 94.)
Either or both	1. The teacher or a student poses two statements, such as, "I love mysteries. I love poetry." 2. Students will form a large outer circle. The teacher visually divides the circle in half, designating one side of the circle for one statement and the other for the second statement. 3. Students move to the side that is true for them. If both statements are true, they stand in the middle of the circle. If neither is true, they stay in their place. 4. Students meet with those who made the same choice to develop reasons for why they feel the way they do or like a certain hobby, for example.

Figure 4.1

Beginning-of-the-Year Survey

Your name: _____ Your birthday: _____

Siblings and ages: _____

Pets: _____

Three things you enjoyed about school last year:

    1. _____

    2. _____

    3. _____

Three things that were a challenge about school last year:

    1. _____

    2. _____

    3. _____

Hobbies or interests outside of school:

_____

_____

_____

Strong likes and dislikes:

_____

_____

_____

Figure 4.2

Venn Diagram Activity

How We're Alike

Directions: Talk with your partner about your life, hobbies, interests, likes, and dislikes. Record things that you have in common in the space where the two circles intersect. Record things that are unique to you in the "Me" circle and things that are unique to your partner in the "You" circle.

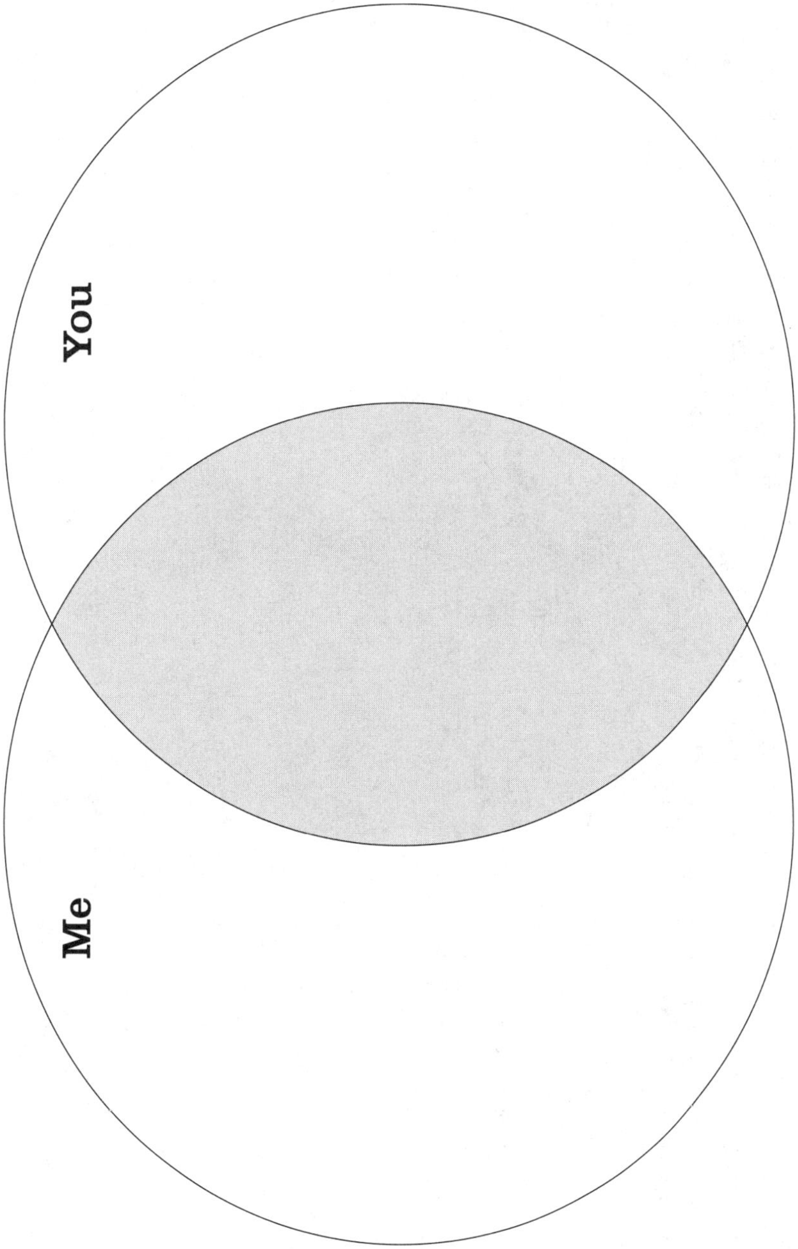

Me

You

Figure 4.3

Three-Question Interview

Directions: Write three questions that you could ask to learn more about classmates. To get the best responses, make sure the questions show genuine interest and are open-ended. Record your questions in the first column. Then, when your teacher directs you, interview three people and record their responses.

Questions	Person 1 Response	Person 2 Response	Person 3 Response
1.			
2.			
3.			

Figure 4.4

Many teachers do a few back-to-school activities for one or two days and then move on, but it is important that these activities go beyond these first days. It is simply impossible even to learn everyone's name in such a short time, much less find out more about them, such as their interests, hobbies, or strengths. Continue to emphasize getting to know each other, even if just for a few minutes each day, for several weeks.

One activity Charlotte especially enjoyed was the two-circle activity. Establishing a set structure, assigned partners and conversation topics, and a clear expectation that everyone would engage with the question with each partner allowed her to experience some success with conversations that she could not find on her own. The structure was one of many over the course of the year that scaffolded the learning of conversational skills, slowly helping her improve her ability to communicate with classmates. With this structure, after students have a chance to talk with several classmates, they report out what they have learned. This sharing out gave Charlotte a productive way to "tell on" classmates.

In these first few weeks, students should also have a chance to plan together and enjoy each other's company, building a sense of shared purpose and joy. For example, they might use class meetings to make plans for what their families should do or experience on Back-to-School Night; make decisions about how to set up the classroom, such as how the classroom library will be organized; engage in fun choral-reading or singing activities; or play community-building games. For more on community building in the first few weeks of school, see the Center for the Collaborative Classroom's Caring School Community program (www .collaborativeclassroom.org/programs/caring-school-community/), which provides daily community-building lesson plans and other resources, and *The First Six Weeks of School* (Responsive Classroom 2015).

Teach Community Expectations

Especially in older grades, it can be tempting to assume that children already know how to behave in a classroom community. But being part of a community is difficult at any age. Students benefit from frequently discussing how to deal with the challenges of classroom life in a way that takes care of themselves and their classmates. This process can begin with students drafting their own rules with teacher guidance or fleshing out existing class norms or rules.

Classroom Norm Making in Action

Over the years of teaching, I was always struck by how powerful it can be to create class norms with students. I remember one year in particular in which my class' work with creating rules together had a yearlong impact on our community.

I began our discussion of rules very generally, asking, "Why do groups even need rules?" We tried to play a game without any rules and laughed at how ridiculous it was. I read a funny book, *What If Everybody Did That?* by Ellen Javernick (2010), which showed some extreme examples of what would happen in a world without rules. My eccentric group of students that year, who, I suspected, might otherwise assert that we didn't even need rules, quickly bought in and were ready to get to work.

The next day I asked students to brainstorm and individually write some rules that would help us have a safe and productive learning environment. Students then shared out. The hodgepodge of rules they created ranged from very idealistic statements to some more practical suggestions. Here are just a few from that list:

➤ Be respectful.

➤ Don't gossip.

➤ Don't save seats for people at lunch.

➤ Listen to the teacher.

➤ Do your best.

➤ Be kind.

After school I wrote each child's contribution on a sentence strip. The next day I gathered the students together and placed the sentence strips in the middle of our circle. Students tried to group rules that went together. This is harder than it sounds and led to many great discussions about what each proposed rule would require of them. For example, students had a very lively conversation about where "Do your best" should go and whether it was even an appropriate rule. They ultimately decided to give it its own category, which eventually became "Take care of yourself," which they fleshed out to mean being kind to oneself, trying to learn as much as one could, and putting oneself in positive situations.

The next day we took the groups of detailed rules students had created and tried to write norms that would cover each group. Again, the class was incredibly engaged with the process. Students had an impassioned discussion about whether "Be respectful" would encompass "Be kind." Some students argued it was impossible to be respectful without being kind, but others argued that kindness requires more of people than being respectful. The class ultimately agreed with the latter argument and wrote the group rule as, "Be respectful and kind." All year they took kindness very seriously. Their initial rule-making discussions prompted many more over the year about what it meant when we explicitly expected classmates to be kind.

{ **strategy** }

Use Class Rules
as an Anchor All Year

Over the course of the first few weeks and throughout the year, you can then extend this work of making rules for students by frequently considering how those rules or norms apply in common classroom situations. Figure 4.5 shows how that work might look.

CREATING NORMS BASED ON CHALLENGING SITUATIONS		
Challenging Situation	**Question**	**What the Discussion Will Help Students Develop**
Talking with a partner for think–pair–share or turn-and-talk	What will it look like to follow our rule "Respect each other" when we do think–pair–share?	• A concrete understanding of respect • The ability to use this academic procedure productively • An understanding of the give-and-take of conversation
Working on a task in small groups	What will you need to do to follow our rule "Take care of classmates" as you do your project?	• Skills for dividing up work fairly • Empathy for those with whom they are working • A beginning understanding of what *care* means in the community

continues

Challenging Situation	Question	What the Discussion Will Help Students Develop
Recess	What would our rules require of you if you saw someone all alone on the playground?	• Connection between rules and action • Compassion for others • Mutual responsibility

Figure 4.5

This intentional work around building and understanding expectations is especially important for students who are struggling to fit in socially. If you don't begin by explicitly naming expectations for and specifics of how to include and care for others, then common strategies such as partnering students or having them work in small groups may actually backfire for the students who struggle. They and their classmates need to know that you expect them to respectfully work with everyone and develop some strategies for how to do that.

{ strategy }

Engage in Daily
Community Meetings

To sustain the work of the first few weeks of school, you should also plan to engage in some type of community gathering each day. Such gatherings extend the work of the first six weeks and of collaborating to build explicit behavior expectations, as they give students a chance to continue to get to know each other, have fun as a group, build social skills in a meaningful setting, and learn at a practical level what it means to follow their classroom rules. These gatherings also infuse joy into a classroom, a by-product that helps both students and us deal with the challenges of school life. The structure for these gatherings can vary, but they often involve one or more of these common elements:

➤ *Greeting each other*: This simple and brief act can go a long way toward building a community, as children are regularly welcomed into the group, hear their and others' names, and at least at that moment are clearly part of the class. Without such a greeting, it's entirely possible that some students might go a whole day or even a week without anyone acknowledging them by name at school.

➤ *Answering a question of the day or discussing a daily prompt*: Such questions or prompts can give students a chance to share their interests, likes and dislikes, family stories, or academic work. When structured well, they not only help students get to know each other but also help all students learn conversational skills they can then transfer to other situations.

➤ *Engaging in a cooperative game or reading or singing experience*: Such shared experiences help students enjoy each other's company in a purposeful and relaxed way. They can also provide opportunities for meaningful social skill practice such as following directions, taking turns, and exercising self-control.

While these meetings benefit all students, they can be especially critical for students like Charlotte. I remember one day in particular when our daily gathering gave her a chance to shine. We were playing a two-minute group game called Dot-to-Dot. Each student had about ten seconds to make dots on the back of a piece of scrap paper. The drawer then passed the paper to the next person, who had about a minute to try to connect the dots into a meaningful picture. There was a great deal of shared laughter as many students and I struggled to make the most basic of pictures from the dots, such as a simple house or a face. When Charlotte shared hers, however, there was silence, as she had taken her partner's dots and drawn a beautiful and detailed parrot. I remember how she brightened at her classmates' obvious admiration and how that small moment slightly elevated her status. It was one of many moments that helped others and Charlotte herself identify her as an artist.

For more on holding daily social gatherings, see the Caring School Community program (www.collaborativeclassroom.org/programs/caring-school-community/), which provides daily community-building lesson plans and other resources, or resources from Responsive Classroom (www.responsiveclassroom.org) or the Origins Program (www.originsonline.org).

Morning Gathering in Action

A few years ago, I had the privilege of working with colleagues at the Center for the Collaborative Classroom on a revision of the Caring School Community program. Our team would write plans for daily class gatherings and then watch teachers pilot those lessons with students. I particularly remember watching a teacher and her sixth-grade students participate in a joyful and productive fifteen-minute meeting to start their day and week. The meeting began as the teacher had the students follow their previously established procedure for quickly moving their chairs to form a circle, in which they sat next to their partners from the prior week. She then told them that they would begin their gathering by greeting each other with a handshake. She modeled how that handshake should look, demonstrating the many skills a good handshake interaction requires—applying gentle but firm contact, shaking the hand for a few seconds but not so long as to be awkward, and maintaining some eye contact during the greeting, just to name a few. Students then passed the handshake around the circle, greeting each other by name as they did so. This brief but happy start took only a few minutes, but in that time, everyone in the circle had his or her name said with respect and experienced a gentle but firm physical encounter with another human being. Although it was a simple activity, it was very moving to watch these sixth-grade students do it so thoughtfully, carefully, and sincerely.

The teacher then assigned students new partners for the week ahead and had students move to sit next to their new partners. Having the same partner for the entire week gave the students the chance to get to know someone more in depth than quick get-to-know-you activities allow. The teacher briefly had students review expectations for how they would treat their partners, tying those to the class norms.

Then the new partners engaged in a quick but meaningful and lively activity called Would You Rather?, in which students explored a question such as "Would you rather listen to music for an hour or watch TV for an hour, and why?" or "Would you rather live in a place that is usually hot or a place that is usually cold, and why?" Students visibly enjoyed themselves as they discussed these questions with partners and then had even more fun posing a few Would You Rather? questions of their own. Every student was engaged and smiling, and the teacher was able to circulate, making brief connections with a few pairs of students.

As an observer, I was so intrigued to see that although some students had begun that Monday visibly tired or grumpy, by the end of the meeting all but one student looked happy and much more energized. Later the teacher shared an observation about a phenomenon I had observed during my own teaching—that even on mornings like that one when it was hard to come back from the weekend and get back into the school groove, the class gathering left her feeling much more centered and excited about the week ahead.

{ strategy }

Foster Inclusion and Compassion

Most of the time, students do not set out to exclude those who struggle to connect, are socially isolated, or have challenging behaviors. Rather, without explicit encouragement or guidance to do otherwise, they just ignore them. Like us, they are just naturally drawn to those with whom they feel an immediate connection, and those are the children they interact with. However, we can take some simple steps to inspire students to develop more empathy and move beyond their comfort zone to look out for classmates who are different or isolated. Consider the following ideas:

➤ **Explicitly name inclusion as a class goal:** Encourage students to pay attention and notice when classmates or students from other classes are sitting by themselves at lunch or walking around the recess yard by themselves. Often just raising students' awareness can spur them to take action. Go beyond this by encouraging them and teaching them how to ask someone to join them at lunch or in a game. Brainstorm common topics to discuss at lunch. Teach them some simple games to play at recess that can include many people.

During Charlotte's school year, we had a class meeting about inclusion. The students agreed that they would begin to look out for people who did not have anyone to play with. It took a few days, but eventually, I noticed a duo of girls "adopt" Charlotte. Although she was not always fully integrated with their elaborate, imaginative games, being able to at least play alongside them and sometimes get what they were doing was a big step for her.

➤ **Teach empathy and compassion:** Having frequent and explicit conversations that require students to think empathetically and compassionately can have a lasting impact on your students and their lives outside the classroom. Literature can provide a great starting place for these discussions. You can also use events that happen in your classroom, at school, or in the local, state, or national community to begin pushing students to think about how other people might feel and what your students might do to help others.

Use Challenging Social Situations as Teachable Moments

Many times throughout the day, such as transitions among classes, recess, lunch, pack-up time, dismissal, and assemblies, are challenging for all students, but especially those who struggle or are isolated. Taking just a few minutes to prepare students for these moments and reflect on successes and challenges afterward can help them both navigate more successfully and over time develop skills they can use throughout the school day. For students who struggle, it can also decrease the likelihood that these challenging times of day will send them into downward spirals or foster self-defeating behaviors.

The following simple structure is particularly effective for setting students up for success during challenging times of day:

1. *Give students a target or goal for the time period.* Take a few minutes before the challenging time period and discuss with students one action they might take during that time. Let them know you will check in with them afterward to see if they tried it and how it worked. For example, you might assign students lunch partners and ask them to find out three things about their partner they didn't already know. Or, before recess, you might ask students to pay attention to people who need help. Before dismissal time, ask students, "How can you take care of people who have a hard time getting organized at dismissal time?"

2. *Have them practice the goal during that time of day.* Set up structures to make sure that students can actually meet the goal. For example, post lunch partners in the cafeteria or accompany your class to the cafeteria to make sure kids find their partners and are sitting with them at the start of lunch.

3. *Reflect on how students did with the target and what they might improve next time.* As soon as possible after the time period, check in with students about how they did. Doing so lets them know that you meant what you said and that they are accountable for acting. Briefly sharing about what students tried also allows students to hear the ways others tried to reach the goal, opening new possibilities for them.

Pair and Group Students
in Varied Ways

Although for purposes of developing their sense of autonomy, you may sometimes want to give students choice about whom to sit or work with, it is also helpful to frequently assign partners, group members, or seats. Doing so requires that students learn how to work with everyone and also ensures that the same students are not repeatedly left with no one wanting to sit with them or be their partners.

It is just as important to switch up seating and pair and group assignments frequently. It is easy for even the most tolerant and skilled students to grow weary and frustrated if they are always paired with students who struggle. In addition, students can develop their skills with working with many different people only if they actually have a chance to do so.

{ strategy }

Notice When Students Are Absent

One of the most powerful signals we can send to students is that we notice when they're gone. When we take note of students who are absent by saying something like, "Oh, I'm going to miss so-and-so today," it shows the students who are present that we value each of them. Similarly, it can be helpful to ask students to be responsible for collecting assignments or remembering key information to share with absent students upon their return.

If students are absent for multiple days, a simple call home to check on them is an easy way to convey how much we care and how much they are missed. Similarly, a warm welcome upon their return takes only a few seconds but expresses a great deal.

Find Ways to Connect Individually

Given our busy school days, it can be hard to connect with students individually, but even a few minutes here and there can go a long way to helping students feel connected to school and to us. A brief smile and check-in with students at the start of the day can make them feel as if they belong in the class and that the day ahead holds new possibilities. You might also find time to talk with students during writing or other lengthy independent work times. Occasionally visiting with students at lunch or recess provides even more meaningful opportunities to see what's happening and to find out what they're interested in.

One way I got to know Charlotte was through my practice of using conversation journals. Every morning students spent about ten minutes writing me a brief message in their little journal (a three-by-five-inch spiral notebook with a ring at the top). I would briefly respond. (Think of it like texting without the phone.) I was always amazed at what I learned from students and what we discussed in these journals. That was how I first learned about Charlotte's love of and knowledge about cats. Having had a lifelong allergy to these creatures, I was able to ask questions that Charlotte found amusingly clueless. She was able to be the expert and share stories of the adventures of her own two cats. Slowly, the notebook and other interactions helped us form a closer bond.

For students you are really struggling to get to know, you might have to go further. Occasionally I would let a child help me with a project while everyone else was at recess. I found that some students opened up more when actually doing a task, like reshelving or labeling books or cleaning off desks. Sometimes I also let students come to the classroom a few minutes early or stay a little longer after school. Again, there was usually some other purpose to the visit, such as helping with a classroom task or working on an assignment together. Whatever the reason, I made it my mission to find out as much as possible about these students at whatever times I could find.

{strategy}

Cultivate Appreciation and Care

Getting to know students is just the first step. The next step is to start appreciating them, learning about their personalities and interests, and ultimately liking and caring for them. It can be helpful to keep a running list of students' positive qualities, their interests, and their hobbies. It also helps to reframe qualities that appear negative at school but might be positive in other settings. For example, being extremely assertive might mean that a child knows how to stand up for himself or others or cares about fairness and justice. Children who frequently tell on others, like Charlotte, care about the rules and in their own ways are trying to show some respect for us and our rules.

Appreciating students for who they are often requires that we step outside our comfort zones—opening ourselves up to new information and experiences. When I was teaching kindergarten, I had a student who was obsessed with the Fast and the Furious movies, frequently writing about them in his journal and mentioning events during class. Even though neither fast cars nor fast-car movies are really my thing, I decided to watch one. I'll never forget the look on that student's face when I told him. When I taught middle school, I listened to all sorts of music my students recommended, even though I probably never would have found my way to any of the artists or songs on my own. Once they realized I was listening, my students would bring more and more song titles for me to try out. It was a relatively easy way to build connections and especially effective for students who struggled. When I was able, I went to students' special events—a traditional dance recital for several students from India, sporting events, and even a few family celebrations. It can be challenging, even uncomfortable sometimes—not to mention time-consuming—to try new things or go new places, but there is no better way to get to know students than to experience something with them.

Of course, you can let children know you appreciate or care for them in simpler ways as well. Ask about a hobby or an event you know they've engaged in. Or consider sending students notes. For example, I tried to occasionally leave little sticky notes on my students' desks or in their homework folders, letting them know that I had seen or noticed something they had done or reported to me. To be sure I didn't overwhelm myself and didn't leave anyone out, I wrote a few of these a day and then distributed them once I was done.

For some students, I literally kept tallies of every time I said something positive or corrective, trying to make sure my ratio favored the former. If I noticed I was trending toward corrective, I would do my best to try to genuinely notice positive behaviors or make more positive connections. See Figure 4.6 for some additional suggestions.

{ commitment }

Learn More About Individual Students

The following exercise from Donald Graves, the great writing instruction guru, is one I have done and recommended for years as a powerful tool for assessing how well I knew my students. To complete the exercise, make and complete a chart like the one on page 111, and then follow the steps below.

- *First column:* List the students you teach. Try not to list them in alphabetical or grade-book order but instead just as they come to you. Then reflect:
  - Who came to mind first? Why do you think this happened?
  - Were there any students you struggled to remember? This could be a sign that you might need to spend more time with them.

- *Second column:* List some things you know about the student, not statistical information (age, how many brothers or sisters, etc.), but personal information. Consider what the child is interested in, what she is passionate about, or what makes her unique. Then reflect:
  - Are there children you know a lot about? How did you develop this knowledge?
  - Was it hard to think of any personal information about some children? Why might this be?

  Now consider your next steps: What will you do to get to know some children better?

- *Third column:* Put a check mark or star next to any interest or passion that you have explicitly discussed with the child. In other words, indicate that the child knows you know about this particular aspect of him. If there are students whose interests and passions you know about but have not communicated about, consider when and how you might talk about those.
  - Repeat this exercise several times throughout the year to keep updated on the progress you are making with fostering strong student relationships.

continues

Student	Interests, Likes, Dislikes, and So On	Have you had an explicit conversation with the child about this interest?

Figure 4.6

{ strategy }

Incorporate Shared and Meaningful Academic Experiences

Academics can often be a powerful route for building community. When students are engaged together in meaningful and interesting work, it can lead to shared bonds and memories. For example, many of my classes have found connection from the experience of reading a book together. Showing my age, I particularly remember the year the first book of J. K. Rowling's Harry Potter series came out. I read it aloud before its fame had grown, and my class loved discussing and acting out the book and later relished in being on the cutting edge of what became a huge literary event. Another year my fifth graders were engrossed in reading R. J. Palacio's book *Wonder* together and would frequently refer to it in their own interactions. Hearing or reading and then discussing a great book together allows students a feeling similar to that of taking a trip or being in an intense experience with someone; it creates a lasting bond.

Similarly, meaningful academic units on important and compelling topics can bring a class together. They can also lead students who might never otherwise find each other to work together. For example, I used to teach a unit that combined math and social studies in which students worked in groups of three to create businesses. They would agree on a product to make or a service to sell and then make a business plan. They would borrow money from the class bank and then have several selling days, keeping track of their sales, repaying their loan, and ultimately taking note of their profit. I was always amazed at the strange bedfellows this unit made. One year, a student who had never before connected with classmates despite my best efforts formed strong ties to his business teammates after they realized that this student had a real knack for budgeting and taking care of money.

As often as possible, try to engage your students with meaningful shared academic experiences, as suggested in Figure 4.7. Even better, incorporate assignments that require students to authentically and meaningfully work together.

{commitment}

Find Opportunities for Relatedness in Your Curriculum

Reflect on these questions to plan next steps for fostering relationships through academics:

- What are you currently doing academically that either is or could be a vehicle for fostering strong student-student and teacher-student bonds?

- How could you enhance existing academic work to more intentionally promote relationships?

- What additional steps might you take?

  - Doing some read-alouds?

  - Creating an integrated study—a unit built around a compelling topic in social studies, science, or the arts?

  - Intentionally incorporating pair or small-group work within existing units?

  - Incorporating meaningful and authentic work within units?

Figure 4.7

{ strategy }

Connect Social
and Academic Learning

Teaching social skills alongside of academics not only strengthens students' relatedness but, for students like Charlotte, who struggle with the social skills needed to connect with others, can also provide them with instruction in these skills and meaningful opportunities to practice them. For example, have students engage in conversations with partners before they discuss a topic as a whole class, taking the time to teach them exactly how such partner conversations should look or sound. Or, in teaching students the skills of academic discourse called for by the Common Core State Standards (CCSS), brainstorm sentence stems to use in those conversations and practice using an appropriate tone for such work. There are innumerable ways that take little extra time but can infuse academic learning with the teaching of social skills. This work helps all students but especially students who find it hard to connect or work with others. Making the skills of such connection explicit ensures that students reap the benefits of this social and academic work and might eventually transfer these skills to other settings.

Consider these strategies for teaching social skills:

* *Model expected behaviors.* Take a few minutes before students will use a needed social skill to model expectations for its use. Seeing a skill in action greatly increases the chance that students can use it.

* *Discuss the skills required.* Ask what students already know about an expected behavior. Bringing key ideas for what students should do clarifies expectations, and having those ideas come from students reinforces the idea that students should act in socially responsible ways, not just to be compliant but because that is what is expected as part of a community. If students miss key ideas, add those, modeling as needed.

* *Refer to previous experiences.* As they are learning social skills, students often demonstrate desired skills in one setting but then fail to transfer them to others. It can help to call out times that

they have succeeded. For example, if students successfully worked in small groups to complete an English language arts task and you are about to have them embark on group work in science, you might lead a reflection by saying something like, "I noticed that you worked very effectively in small groups yesterday to complete your character charts. Almost everyone was on task, listening to others, and contributing to the group's work. What helped you be successful? How can that help you with our science project?"

➤ *Chart key expectations.* For more challenging or new social skills, it can be helpful to create a visual of key expectations. For example, for kindergarten students, post a photo of two students sitting knee-to-knee and making eye contact as a helpful reminder of how to have a partner conversation. For older students, collaboratively make and frequently return to a chart detailing the key steps in active listening to help them put this advanced skill to use.

For all of these strategies, remember to help students reflect afterward about how well they applied the social skill.

Teaching Social and Academic Skills in Action

A teacher I observed once led a simple but powerful lesson on both academics and working with a partner. Academically, students were working on identifying the narrative elements in stories they were reading and putting those elements to work in their own writing. After students had read many books together and identified their settings, plots, and characters as well as analyzed how these elements interacted, she wanted to challenge students to begin putting these elements to use in their own writing. She put students in pairs and then gave each pair a different wordless picture book. Their first task was simply to look through the book and try to figure out what the story and its elements were.

Before sending students off to complete this task, however, the teacher took just a few minutes to set them up for success with the social skills involved. She said, "Our rules say we need to take care of each other. How can you take care of each other while looking through your book?" Students responded that they could make sure they each got to equally hold and see the book, they could check in to see if their partner was ready to turn the page before doing so, and they could use the class sentence stems ("I think _____ because _____" and "I disagree with

_____ because _____") to explain their thinking about what was happening in the book.

As students worked, the teacher mingled, reinforcing ways students were using what they knew about stories to make sense of the text and how they were working with partners. One pair was having a particularly hard time, arguing about both small issues, such as when to turn the pages, and larger ones, such as what their assigned story meant. The teacher stopped and sat with them a minute, guiding them to make better decisions about sharing the resource and helping them use the sentence frames as well as evidence from the book to guide their discussion. By the time she left them, they were, if not completely friendly, at least encountering some success.

At the end of the session, the teacher facilitated a brief reflection on students' academic experience and their social experience. First she asked, "How did you determine what the story and narrative elements were in your text?" She then asked, "What did you do well in terms of taking care of your partners?"

The teacher's interweaving of social and academic learning not only set her students up for success with a meaningful task but also helped make her own inter-actions with students more productive and joyful. Rather than putting out small fires, as many teachers do during such partner work, the teacher for the most part was able to have positive interactions with students. Use Figure 4.8 to plan for how you might integrate social and academic learning. Even with the pair to which she had to offer more support, her prework provided a structure on which they could build and a set of shared understandings about her expectations that helped that pair improve. She was able to intervene quickly and successfully, bolstering her own sense of competence and helping her maintain her equanimity.

{commitment}

Teach the Social Skills Your Students Need

To purposefully integrate the teaching of social skills, reflect on what social skills your students most need, where they need those, and how you can teach them.

Social Skills My Students Need	How I Know: What the Students Are Currently Saying or Doing That Shows a Need	When They Most Need to Use the Skills for Academic Tasks	How I Can Teach the Skills to Set Students Up for Success with the Task

Figure 4.8

For a helpful list of social and emotional skills, see the core competencies of the Collaborative for Academic, Social, and Emotional Learning (https://casel.org/core-competencies/).

section
05

Competence

{ difficulty }

Ricardo Gave Up Before Trying

From almost our first day together, one of my kindergarten students, Ricardo, found it hard to get started on almost anything I asked him to do. At center time, even a seemingly straightforward task, such as one in which students stamped the letters of their name with rubber stamps and an ink pad, led him to cry out, "I can't do it!" If he did start a task, he would give up almost immediately if he didn't encounter success, frequently with a great deal of tears and physical agitation. For example, when he couldn't at first ride our outdoor bikes, he kicked one, crying, "I can't do it. It's stupid!" At such moments, he almost seemed to be in a panic, with his fight-or-flight instinct in high gear.

His outbursts scared many of his classmates, who, upon trying to reassure or help him, were often met with an emotional outburst or a physical response. While he loved several parts of the kindergarten day, especially read-alouds, Ricardo obviously felt

118

overwhelmed by much of what he was expected to do. Interestingly, it was hard for me as his teacher to understand his response. He was actually very capable and often, if I could get him to try something, he would catch on quickly. But he did not recognize his own competence.

While Ricardo's questioning of his own competence was extreme, his need to feel and be competent was not. All students need to feel and be able to show that they are capable, that they have useful skills and knowledge that allow them to meaningfully contribute to their school and wider communities. When students feel this sense of competence at school, they become more engaged with their classmates and teachers and what they are learning. And even a little taste of feeling or being competent can fuel students' desire to feel more of it. They begin to see work on their relationships with peers and teachers and work at academics as more worthwhile, increasing their motivation and effort.

Students who feel competent at school do better socially and academically. They feel more secure and confident, which in turn frees them up to take risks and try new and challenging tasks. Feelings of competence give them social confidence as well, freeing them from the judgment of others to make sound choices about whom to interact with and how to do so. On the other hand, students who don't feel competent at school often act in negative and unproductive ways. As an astute educator once said, "Students would rather appear bad than stupid." In other words, if they are lacking a sense of competence, they would rather break rules and go against class norms than show classmates and teachers that they struggle in a given area. The work we do to bolster students' sense of competence will have both short- and long-term positive consequences for students, our classroom communities, and us.

It is important not to see supporting students in building competence as just another thing to do, like so much in our lives as teachers, but as an essential part of what we do. Moreover, ensuring that every child learns to be good and feel good at one if not many things can happen within the structures of what we already do. We can look at any lesson or any series of lessons, any play or choice experience, and think about whether or not it moves every student on a continuum toward competence. And if it does not, we can make adjustments so that the instruction conforms to the needs of the student, not the other way around.

Specifically, in this chapter we discuss the following ways to build students' competence:

➜ providing many and varied opportunities for students to feel competent

➜ helping students find or develop feelings of competence

➜ using our language to foster feelings of competence

➜ teaching students to reflect and self-assess

We also need to become more aware of ways we, even unconsciously, undermine students' sense of competence and be more intentional about our treatment of and feedback for students.

{ shift }

Provide Multiple Opportunities to Develop Competence

One challenge school presents is its fairly narrow view of competence—in most school settings, competence is defined as the ability to do academic tasks well, which, in turn, is often defined as getting good grades. But children can and should experience feelings of competence in multiple areas—cognitive knowledge and skills, including those that they have developed outside of school; physical skills and accomplishments; social success; and emotional strengths. One way to help students feel such competence is to broaden the scope of how we define it and be on the lookout for ways we can offer opportunities in all areas for students to grow and succeed and to recognize or help them recognize when they do so.

Many students have the potential to develop great expertise or skill; they're just looking for the opportunity to discover those things. Offering a wide range of academic experiences, such as opportunities to write across genres, express themselves artistically, or actively do science, can open students to possible skill areas they wouldn't otherwise know about. Similarly, exploring meaningful topics and helping students discover topics of personal interest through reading and other experiences can help get them excited and develop expertise on a topic.

That is what Gianna did with the student she discussed in Section 2, Willy. William Carlos Williams' poetry, to which Willy so deeply connected, offered a natural link to teaching about tense, a fifth-grade standard. Williams might have already eaten the plums, but he was presently asking for forgiveness. Gianna taught Willy to notice this difference in tense choice. He became intrigued and began to look for those tense decisions while reading and make thoughtful decisions about the tenses he used in his own writing. Every time he recognized or intentionally used tense appropriately, it was a success. Over time Willy became a tense expert, enabling Gianna to say to the class, "If anyone needs help proofreading for tense, you can make an appointment with Willy."

Be alert for times when students demonstrate such potential for competence. Point out successes to students and look for ways that competence on one task can build toward competence on another.

Figure 5.1 gives some picture of what competence can look like in four areas and suggests ways to incorporate into our current work the different opportunities that might lead to competency.

EXPERIENCES THAT FOSTER COMPETENCE			
Physical Competence	**Cognitive Competence**	**Social Competence**	**Emotional Competence**
Catching a ball, making a pass, or scoring a goal	Selecting and using an efficient math strategy for problem solving	Giving meaningful social advice to a friend	Losing a game at recess without getting overly upset
Publishing a beautifully designed and illustrated writing piece	Analyzing a character's development and change in a book	Organizing a recess soccer game	Completing a challenging math assignment despite initially being stumped
Performing in a play, concert, or dance	Finishing a challenging book	Inviting someone else to play and then enjoying that time	Using a self-soothing strategy when feeling upset
Making a painting	Writing a poem	Giving another person a sincere and meaningful compliment	Recognizing that someone else's feelings have been hurt and checking on that person
Conducting a science experiment	Solving a riddle	Contributing meaningfully to a group project	Taking a short break from an academic assignment when feeling frustrated

Figure 5.1

Of course, these areas overlap. When students experience competence in the physical realm, they might also experience cognitive, social, and even emotional competence. We need to take a broad view of students' need for competence and act accordingly.

Often making small adjustments to what we already do can open up possibilities in these areas. For example, having students work in pairs on certain academic tasks can lead to feelings of cognitive competence as students learn new information together or successfully complete a task. Such an opportunity can also foster feelings of social competence, as students work cooperatively together. And it can give children a chance to successfully cultivate positive emotions or regulate their emotions.

For school opportunities to foster students' sense of competence, however, we have to carefully think through each aspect of the project, lesson, or activity and how to foster students' success. For example, when pairing students for partner work, consider each partner's needs—on a math task, it can diminish the sense of competence a student who struggles with math feels if she is paired with a student who is extraordinarily advanced in math. Similarly, to feel socially competent, students often need us to do some preteaching of expected social skills and put structures in place to support partner work. However, with little additional effort, we can plan to support feelings of competence not just academically but in the other realms as well.

Ricardo had a great deal of cognitive competence and struggled particularly with physical competence—feeling challenged when asked to stamp letters, write his name, or ride a bike. When planning tasks with a physical component, I began to look for ways for him to show that he cognitively understood tasks even if he doubted his ability to physically complete them. For example, when we began writing, I would often have him (and other students) orally rehearse what he wanted to say first, sometimes even recording it for him. When Ricardo saw that he had something to say in writing, it was easier for him to take on the physical challenge of actually doing so.

Expanding Opportunities to Build Competence in Action

My sixth- and seventh-grade English language arts students were developing their skills with opinion writing by learning to write evidence-based reviews. We began with restaurant reviews. Students worked in pairs to read and analyze the qualities of exemplary restaurant reviews. Then we took a walk to a nearby restaurant, and students worked with the same partners to evaluate the restaurant on a variety of factors identified from their review of the exemplars. When we returned to school, students then individually wrote their own reviews. They shared them with their partners and gave and received feedback on their work. Finally, they revised them, and we published them in a class book, which we made available to others in the school.

Although writing was the central focus of this series of lessons, this work offered numerous opportunities for students to develop other competencies. I tried to do some intentional planning to support that development, as shown in the Figure 5.2.

PLANNING FOR COMPETENCE	
Area of Competence	**How I Cultivated Skills**
Cognitive	• The assignment fostered a wide range of cognitive skills, such as the ability to disaggregate the strong elements of the exemplary reviews, the ability to gather and record evidence at the restaurant, and the ability to synthesize that evidence and write a strong and compelling review. • At each stage I sought to foster students' sense of competence by noting particular tasks they did well ("Many of you were able to generalize from several reviews to find common elements. That shows analytical thinking"). • I also frequently sought to help them prepare themselves to perform well ("How will you organize your notes at the restaurant?") or reflect on their own performance ("Which three elements of strong restaurant reviews did you include?").

continues

Area of Competence	How I Cultivated Skills
Physical	• Students who wanted to could add drawings to their notes at the restaurant or add illustrations to their published reviews. • The restaurant was not that far, but many of my students did not walk much in their everyday lives, so we were able to talk about stamina and how well the students did with that while going to and coming from the restaurant. For some, that physical accomplishment proved more important than I had anticipated.
Social	• I explicitly taught social expectations, such as how to share ideas with a partner in reading the exemplars and at the restaurant and how to give a partner feedback on his or her draft. • I asked students to reflect on their work with partners throughout the process. • On several occasions, I had to step in to provide support for partnerships when students struggled. However, with that support, they could be successful and were very excited and proud at the end of the project.

continues

Area of Competence	How I Cultivated Skills
PLANNING FOR COMPETENCE *continued*	
Emotional	• I had one student who frequently became easily upset at seemingly small setbacks or loud noises. We did some work in advance to prepare him for the restaurant and develop a list of strategies for him to use if he started feeling anxious. • Students frequently reflected on how they dealt with setbacks and problems. For example, I asked, "What have you been doing to stay in control of your emotions when you have felt frustrated by or disagreed with your partner?" • The project also offered many moments when students were visibly excited and happy. Sometimes it can be powerful for students to reflect on what leads to such positive emotions, so I said, "You all had such a great time and looked so happy at the restaurant. What happened to cause those feelings?"

Figure 5.2

Use Figure 5.3 that follows to also assess a child's strengths.

{commitment}

Assess a Child's Strengths

Think of one or more students who are struggling at school, particularly in terms of feeling competent. Do a strengths assessment for the students using Figure 5.1 as a guide. Record specific areas of competence for each student:

Child	Physical Competence	Cognitive Competence	Social Competence	Emotional Competence

Then analyze your school day or specific assignments and tasks to look for ways to build in opportunities for students to demonstrate their competencies.

Subject Area or Project	Physical Competence	Cognitive Competence	Social Competence	Emotional Competence
Daily community gathering				
English/ language arts				
Math				
Social studies				
Science				

Figure 5.3

Use Language
That Fosters Competence

Many students go through each school day having their need to feel competence met. They find both the academic and the social life of school relatively easy. They might even excel in other areas, such as sports, adding physical competence to their already long list of successes. We should, of course, care for these students and give them positive feedback, but our priority needs to be students who have the opposite experience. We need to develop frequent and productive ways to offer students who consistently feel like failures at school a more positive lens on their abilities and potential.

The language we use with these students is especially critical. They need to hear about how they are doing, especially their strengths and the progress they are making. They need *information* about their progress, however, not just our opinions. As a result, we need to avoid meaningless praise, such as "You are so smart!" or "You are such an awesome student," as that does nothing to give the child information. Such words might feel good in the moment but do not do anything to help the child feel that he is capable. Indeed, sometimes, particularly with older students, such empty praise has the opposite effect, as students see it as fake and a sign of how much we pity them. Try some of these strategies to offer feedback that will lead to feelings of increased competence:

➤ *Pay attention to strengths.* That old expression "What we pay attention to grows" is true. When we look and listen for seeds of students' competence to reinforce and then do so, those seeds will grow. For some children it can be hard to find them, but we must. If necessary, start small: look for a kind word; appreciate a reflective comment in a class discussion, even if presented out of turn; point out when a child puts a strategy that you have taught to use; or notice a child paying sustained attention for a longer amount of time than he has previously been able to accomplish.

In addition to the benefits to the child, I found that when I started forcing myself to look for positives, my view of children slowly changed, as did my feelings about teaching. Over time I became more and more adept at seeing successes and shifting away from a deficit model. Your enjoyment of your work will increase as you spend more of your days noticing and commenting on what is going well instead of obsessing over what students aren't doing.

→ *Use evidence-based statements to point out successes.* Some children are so self-critical that they don't even recognize when they have done something well. Train yourself to pay attention to their successes, even small ones, so that you can help them see what they have done and can do. Give them information about these accomplishments or the knowledge they are developing:

> → "You have really learned a lot about how to care for animals. All your reading and reflecting have really paid off."

> → "You read that paragraph so well that I could really imagine what the scene looked like."

> → "When you were feeling frustrated with math, you tried one of the calming strategies we discussed, and I saw that it worked. You got right back to the problem and solved it."

→ *Focus on a child's agency and possibility for growth.* Of course, children also need information when they are making mistakes. Just because they need to increase their sense of competence does not eliminate this need. But we can deliver constructive feedback in ways that convey a message of competence by following three rules:

1. Deliver information about mistakes as factually as possible.

2. When appropriate, explain why the mistake matters by tying it to shared values or goals.

3. When needed, help the child reflect on what she can do to address the mistake or avoid the problem in the future.

Here are some examples of such feedback in action:

> → "Your paragraph lacks a topic sentence, so as a reader I had a hard time figuring out what it was about and how these ideas connected. Do you want to try to write that on your own, or would you like some help with it?"

- "You forgot to show the steps of your work for this math problem. It's important to show your work as it allows you to do a better job when you go back to check your answers. It also helps me as a teacher know how you're approaching problems. And, when you get to advanced math, you'll need to be in this habit. So, for these two problems, go back and show how you got the answer."

- "You called Brianna an 'idiot' and 'stupid.' Those are unkind and harsh words. In our class rules, we agreed to treat each other with kindness and respect. What can you do to make amends with her, and what can you do next time you feel frustrated with a science partner instead of using such words?"

- *Point out growth and change.* Researchers Carol Dweck (2007) and Peter Johnston (2004) have found that when we use language that fosters students' understanding of how their actions are leading to their success, we can over time help those students develop their sense of competence and their willingness to embrace new challenges. We can help students develop what Dweck (2007) calls a growth mind-set, a belief that with teaching and strategically applied effort, they can get better or more competent in a given area, by pointing out how their use of specific strategies led to success. Dweck contrasts the growth mind-set with a fixed mind-set, a belief that success derives solely from innate qualities. She points out that even if well-intentioned, feedback like "You are so smart" or "You are the best!" can foster that fixed mind-set. Instead, tie students' success to what you see them doing. Here are some examples of that language in action:

  - "You highlighted key words in these word problems and took the time to figure out exactly what it was asking. Then you carefully did the math. You're becoming quite a mathematician."

  - "I saw that you reread that paragraph several times and stopped to try to figure out several tricky words. That helped you understand the information the author was trying to convey and to contribute to our discussion about it."

→ "I could see that you were getting upset in our class discussion, but I also saw you looking at the chart with our sentence starters. You stayed calm as you said, 'I respectfully disagree with what everyone has said because _____.' You are learning how to control your emotions and have productive academic conversations."

Johnston (2004) discusses the importance of pointing out students' learning histories and showing them the progress they are making, which can sometimes be invisible to students who struggle. For example, you might say:

→ "Remember how at the beginning of the year you had trouble waiting your turn in our classroom conversations? Today you only interrupted a classmate once during that Socratic seminar."

→ "You used to find fractions impossible, but look at this: you got all but two of these problems correct."

→ "Earlier in the year, your paragraphs had only a few sentences and the ideas sometimes didn't connect. Look at what you just wrote. You have a strong topic statement that makes me want to keep reading, and all of these sentences develop that main idea."

→ *Use a genuine and authentic tone of voice.* As we discussed in Section 3, the tone in which we offer feedback is crucial. Avoid overselling positive feedback: when we use an awkwardly elevated tone, the message we unconsciously give is that we are surprised at a child's success—we didn't think she had it in her. Or that tone can convey how much we know the child needs to hear some positive feedback, which again can highlight deficits instead of strengths. It helps to strive for the same tone we would use if we were complimenting a friend or colleague—genuine, authentic, and admiring. Similarly, when you need to give corrective feedback, keep an even, just-the-facts tone, not one that implies disappointment or resignation.

→ *Recognize approximation.* Students who are doing well in all four areas of competence aren't the only ones who should feel skilled. Instead, we need to pay attention to students' approximations, or the small gains they are making even if they are still far from where we'd ultimately like them to be.

Think of Vygotsky's zone of proximal development and scaffolding. For example, even though Gianna's student Willy was in fifth grade, the quality of his writing was what a developing second grader might produce. She could have said, "Willy, all the other fifth graders are writing six completely original poems that have been revised multiple times for line breaks, language specificity, tense, and imagery. In my class we are all held to the same standards." But, obviously, that would not have helped him feel the competence he'd need to keep going with writing. Instead, Gianna focused on the aspects of poetry Willy was doing well, such as being precise with his language. She pointed out examples of this precision and then over time noticed new areas of growth with writing.

Use the language in Figure 5.4 to foster students' sense of competence.

{commitment}

Rehearse Language That Promotes Confidence

It can be helpful to plan and practice language that can foster students' sense of competence. Think of a student whose sense of competence you want to nurture. Use the following table to plan for language you can use in that effort.

Strategy for Increasing Competence	Plan for Opportunities to Provide Feedback	Plan for Language to Use
Pay attention to strengths.	• Where is the child currently demonstrating strengths? • Why do these strengths matter (for the child, the class, etc.)? How can you tie your feedback to these reasons?	
Use evidence-based statements to point out successes.	• When is a time of day or activity in which the child might demonstrate success so that you can observe and take notes?	

continues

Strategy for Increasing Competence	Plan for Opportunities to Provide Feedback	Plan for Language to Use
Focus on a child's agency and possibility for growth.	• When does the child struggle or make mistakes? • Why is it important that the child improve or correct mistakes in this area? • How can you help the child think productively about what to do differently the next time the situation arises?	
Point out growth and change.	• What are some areas in which you hope to see growth? • What will that growth look like? How will you know when you see it?	
Use a genuine and authentic tone of voice.	• Think about the current tone of voice you use in talking with the child. What do you want to change or keep the same?	
Recognize approximation.	• For areas in which the student struggles, what might be some early signs of success you could point out?	

© 2019 by Gianna Cassetta and Margaret Wilson from *The Caring Teacher*. Portsmouth, NH: Heinemann.

Figure 5.4

{strategy}

Teach Students to Reflect and Self-Assess

Although positive and constructive feedback from us, family members, and peers is critical for students to feel competent, we also have to ensure that they learn to accurately assess their own performance and development. True feelings of competence come from being able to reflect on what we have done and decide for ourselves if we did it well or might need to do it differently next time. The ability to self-assess also keeps students from feeling dependent on others for their sense of self-worth. Some ways to foster reflection and students' ability to accurately assess their progress include the following:

➔ *Make reflection a class habit.* One quick way to foster the ability to self-assess is to frequently have the class as a whole reflect on how they did during a particular time of day or on a particular task. Children often find this whole-class reflection to be an easier starting place than looking at their own individual performance. A few minutes at the end of key learning chunks, recess, or social times of day can help students understand what reflection looks like and how to judge their performance. Figure 5.5 shows some examples of such reflection questions in action:

	REFLECTION QUESTIONS IN ACTION	
Situation	**Reflection Question**	**Area of Competence That's Highlighted**
At the end of writing time	What did you do well today in terms of incorporating evidence into your writing?	Cognitive
After a game in PE or recess	How did you do with developing your soccer skills today?	Physical
At the end of a class meeting	How did you stay positive during our discussion, especially the challenging parts?	Emotional
After students work with partners on a science experiment	What did you do well in terms of sharing the materials and work with your partner?	Social

Figure 5.5

➔ *Encourage individual reflection and problem solving.* Children also need chances to think about their own work in whatever area of competency they have experienced—both what they have done well and what they might improve. Frequently encourage students to

   ➔ check their assignments before handing them in;

   ➔ compare their completed assignments against established expectations;

+ write down three things that they did well in a particular area; and

+ set goals for what they might improve the next time they tackle a task or for a whole period of time.

Also think about how to handle students who frequently bring you work with either a spoken question about how they did ("Look at my story; what do you think?") or unspoken doubt, expecting you to judge how they did at a particular task. Sometimes you might just want to use the guidelines listed previously to give them feedback. But often these moments present chances for self-reflection. Take advantage of such opportunities by asking questions such as these:

+ What do you think you did well?

+ What would you say about this work if you were the teacher? Why?

+ What do you like about how you did?

+ What are you proud of about [your performance in a concert, a piece of writing, your work with a friend]?

+ *Provide students with structures and measures by which to judge their performance.* Of course, reflection is only powerful if those doing the reflecting know what success looks like. Whenever possible, provide students a vision or exemplar of what they're aiming for and then have them reflect on their approximation to that goal. For both social and emotional competencies, it can help to post or have on hand reference charts that detail what a certain activity looks like, sounds like, and feels like, such as the one in Figure 5.6, which was created with input from a group of third graders.

WHAT DOES BEING A GOOD PARTNER . . .		
Look Like?	**Sound Like?**	**Feel Like?**
• Listening to a partner's ideas	• Using a kind tone of voice	• Happy
• Sharing ideas	• Listening silently	• Relaxed
• Sharing materials	• Asking, "What do you think?"	• The feeling you get from getting things done
• Taking turns	• Asking, "Would you like to go first?"	• Satisfying
• Working together when needed	• Saying, "You did that really well."	
• Checking with a partner before adding something to a group poster or project	• Saying, "That's a great idea!"	
• Making eye contact when talking	• Asking, "How can we make sure we are doing about the same amount of the work?"	
• Smiling or nodding to show agreement or encouragement		

Figure 5.6

For academic tasks, checklists and rubrics can help students evaluate their work when used effectively, such as those shown in Figure 5.7. As with any tools, students need to learn exactly how to use these. In addition, students need to learn to look for growth, not perfection, when evaluating their work using rubrics and checklists.

{ commitment }

Plan Opportunities for Students to Self-Assess

Consider how you are already providing students opportunities to self-assess and when and how you can expand those opportunities.

	What You Are Currently Doing	**When and How You Might Enhance Your Practice in This Area**
Opportunities for class reflection and self-assessment		Have the class reflect on one or more of these areas of performance: _____ cognitive _____ physical _____ emotional _____ social
Opportunities for individual reflection and problem solving		Teach or provide opportunities for students to _____ check their assignments before handing them in _____ compare their work against established expectations _____ write down three things that they did well in a particular area _____ set goals for what they might improve the next time they tackle a task or for a whole period of time
Structures and measures by which students can judge their performance		Use tools like the following: _____ "Looks Like, Sounds Like, Feels Like" charts _____ exemplars _____ rubrics _____ checklists

Figure 5.7

section
06

Autonomy

{ difficulty }

Alfred Was Seeking Control

Alfred was a second-grade student who was often teary and upset at school and also sought to exert control over classmates and me in seemingly small ways that nonetheless often left us feeling annoyed with him and damaged his relationships. If I asked the class to line up for recess, he would do so but would walk as slowly as possible, making everyone wait on him. When we sang songs or recited poems and used movements to accompany those, he would vary his movements in small but noticeable ways. He would frequently lean into a classmate's personal work area, and when that child asked him to move away, he would, but only slightly. Over time I learned that Alfred's family had faced multiple challenges already in his short life, and I came to suspect that many of these small actions could possibly be ways to exert some much-needed control and order in his life at school.

140

As with all children who struggle, Alfred was not magically transformed over the course of second grade, but he did improve, in part, I think, because he began to feel some autonomy and sense of control over the school part of his life. At the beginning of second grade, as I was establishing routines and teaching them how to do school, students often had few choices and worked on the same assignments. However, as the year went on, I more and more frequently incorporated choice at independent work times. While I met with small reading groups, for example, other students had a list of literacy-related options from which to choose, all tied to key learning goals. Alfred was visibly happier when he had such choices and at least for this time of day was often so engrossed in what he was doing that he did not bother with classmates or interrupt my group work.

{ shift }

Intentionally Cultivate Students' Autonomy

Fostering student autonomy is essential to building strong relationships with students and helping students who struggle begin to thrive socially and academically at school. But it can be hard for us as teachers. Much of our educational tradition is based on a sort of "my way or the highway" approach to teaching. We are used to having or at least trying to have total control in our classrooms. I would even venture to say that many of us were drawn to teaching because we so value planning and controlling things ourselves. That is one reason that we often advocate for autonomy for our profession.

To give students needed autonomy does not require that we completely turn the classroom over to them, but it does mean that whenever possible, we should look for ways to share responsibility and decision making and increase student voice. For many of us, this can be a harder shift to make than those required for helping students meet their needs for relatedness and competence, but it is equally important.

While all my students benefited from my efforts to help them feel autonomous, I especially remember how much students who felt a lack of control in their lives outside of school did. Some students feel a lack of control because so much of their personal lives has been characterized by trauma and chaos. For others, the lack of control comes from the overscheduling of their lives and lack of choice about the path their life will take.

In many ways, it might be easiest for us as teachers to relate to the importance of autonomy to students' well-being at school. How many times in the past few years have we felt those above us and outside our schools were trying to control us, removing our ability to make decisions we felt would better serve our students? Try to tap into the sense of frustration and powerlessness from those moments to better understand how school can feel for your students. It can be scary to give up some of the control we exercise in our classrooms, but doing so has such rewards for our students. It is worth our own temporary discomfort.

{ strategy }

Gradually Share Responsibility

It can be helpful to think of the school year as a continuum of autonomy and responsibility. At the beginning of the year when students are new to each other and your class, you may want to exert more control. You might, for instance, decide where students will sit for each period in class or even at lunch. You might allow students to use the restroom at only certain times when you can supervise their visits. Or you might restrict students from full use of areas of the classroom, such as the classroom library, until you can teach them your expectations for those areas.

However, almost from the start, you should also have in mind the need to teach students how to act responsibly in these and other areas so that over time you can give them more freedom and control. Teach them, for instance, what it means to make a responsible choice about whom to sit with. Practice what that looks like. Have frequent discussions about how to take care of the restroom and others in the restroom and how to prioritize returning to class. Break down your expectations for how to treat each area of the classroom, and teach those to students. Strive to help students have as much control as they demonstrate that they can handle. See Figure 6.1.

If, after you give students responsibility, they have trouble handling it, you can always take some control back. Don't give up on them, however. Evaluate what went wrong, and do some additional teaching.

{commitment}

Shift Ownership to Students

Choose two areas where you currently exercise all the decision making in your classroom. Make a plan for how you can shift some ownership to students. Remember that you can still set parameters, but strive in these two areas to allow students more autonomy and control.

_____ where to work (at desks, sitting, standing, etc.)

_____ whom to work or sit with

_____ how to organize desks or work spaces

_____ what work to display on classroom displays or how to display it

_____ when to use the restroom

_____ how desks or work areas are arranged

_____ how the classroom library is organized or when or how to use it

_____ what to do at free times: during indoor recess, when work is finished, and so on

_____ other: _____

How will you give students more autonomy in these two areas?

_____

_____

_____

Figure 6.1

{strategy}

Involve Students in Class Decision-Making

One straightforward way to help students feel more autonomy and more invested in school is to include them in class decision making. Such inclusion might be small, such as merely asking for student input on decisions. For example, you might ask students for ideas on how to organize the classroom library. Or you could include all students or a few student representatives in discussions of schoolwide issues such as how to prevent bullying, increase safety, or make school improvements.

I remember one year when our school was undergoing the accreditation process, and the accreditation committee visiting our school had a series of conversations with students. It helped them feel as if they had a real and valuable say about what happened at their school. It can be so empowering for us to show that we're at least somewhat interested in students' opinions.

Moving beyond mere input, students can also, with guidance, make decisions about many classroom issues and events. Doing so helps them feel the sense of control that they so need. It also teaches them important social skills, such as how to think critically and rationally in decision making, how to compromise, and how to reach consensus.

One way to make decisions as a class is through structured class meetings. Some decisions students can tackle at such meetings include the following:

- what to do at a class celebration
- how to organize a certain part of the classroom or a classroom display
- what activities to do with a buddy classroom
- what to display or share with parents on Back-to-School or Open House Night
- what to showcase or perform at a schoolwide assembly
- a service project or cause to accomplish as a class

The structure for these meetings is simple and can be adapted for many different decisions and purposes:

1. Introduction

2. Topic

3. Suggestions

4. Decision

5. Conclusion

Here is what happens at each step:

1. **Introduction:** At your first class meeting, you'll need to discuss what a class meeting is and establish meeting rules. Some teachers choose to make specific meeting rules while others choose to use their class rules and discuss how those might apply to class meetings. Here is a set of rules one of my classes decided upon:

   → Speak and listen respectfully, using our prompts.

   → Share specifics but without naming names or accusing anyone.

   → Consider everyone's needs, not just your own.

   After the year is under way, revisit the rules as needed. For some classes, I had to do this at almost every meeting because we struggled with group discussions, particularly about contentious issues. Other classes only needed an occasional reminder.

2. **Topic:** Introduce the decision to be made or the event to be planned together. As you share, be clear about the parameters of the decision students will make. What are the goals of the particular project or event students should strive to address as they consider options and make a decision? What will students have input in, and what aspects are off the table? For example, if students are helping to decide what parents will do or learn at Back-to-School Night, you might share what the goals of the night are—to help parents understand what students will be learning and doing this year in school and to foster a sense of comfort and

community among parents. You can return to these goals as needed later in the meeting to guide students' suggestions and decisions. You might then explain that you have a mostly completed presentation to share with families about what students will learn but want students to decide what parents will do as a community-building activity, what work or activity students will have on their desks for families to see, or what graphics you might use in your presentation. The sense of autonomy that class meetings develop can be undermined if students, unaware of larger goals or limitations, make suggestions or decisions that you then have to reject. It is best to be up-front about constraints.

Once you have introduced the decision and its parameters, you may want to explore what the children already know about this area or what their experience has been. For example, if asking students to decide on activities for families at Back-to-School Night, you might want to find out what students recall from their preparation for similar family events in the past. If planning a class celebration, you might ask, "What sorts of things have you done at parties or celebrations you've attended?"

If you know or suspect that the decision involves an area with which students have no experience, you might offer some ideas of what might happen or what you or past classes have done or planned. For the Back-to-School Night decision, for instance, you might share a few activities you have had parents do in the past to get students' thinking started.

3. **Suggestions:** Invite students to think about their ideas for what to do with regard to the decision at hand. To foster the widest sense of autonomy, use structures that will encourage all students' engagement. You might have students first discuss ideas in pairs or small groups or go around the circle and let everyone contribute ideas. Take notes or chart students' suggestions so long as those fit within the classroom norms you have established and the goals for the event or decision. If a student suggests something that appears to go against the norms or goals, either state that directly or ask the child a question to help him or her self-evaluate.

4. **Decision:** Guide students to decide among the options by using a consensus-building approach. Although consensus building often takes longer than a simple majority vote, such an approach fosters autonomy because it emphasizes that everyone's ideas, opinions, and feelings matter. In contrast, deciding by majority rule leaves many students feeling as if they have no voice or control, undermining their sense of autonomy. Majority rule can be especially problematic because students with more social power can often use that to sway others to vote their way on issues.

   You can build consensus in numerous ways. One is to have students identify their top one to three options on a list of suggestions. You can do this simply, just by putting tally marks next to each option. Or you could give students three colored dots and have them take turns placing them next to their top options. If you are concerned about some in the group exercising too much influence over others, you could also take a break from the meeting and have students write their preferred options privately.

   Once students have identified their preferences, you can start eliminating options with the least student backing. Continue with the process if needed to whittle the list down more. Once the list is down to the final few, you might want to have students speak for or against certain options. Or it sometimes works to propose that the class consider whether there is a way to make the final few options all work. Some teachers use a process of having students show a thumb up for their preference among the final few, thumb in the middle if it's not a preference but an option they could live with, and thumb down if they would have a hard time accepting that option. The teacher then evaluates the results to suggest the consensus.

5. **Conclusion:** End the meeting by summing up the students' decision and what should happen next. Reflect on how students did with the meeting rules or norms. After students have made and carried out the decision, consider meeting again to have students reflect on how it went and what they might do differently next time. Such reflections help improve their decision-making skills and

also further develop a sense of autonomy by letting students know that their opinions and evaluation matter. For more on involving students in decision making, see the Caring School Community program (www.collaborativeclassroom.org/programs/caring -school-community/), which provides class meeting lesson plans and other resources.

Decision-Making Class Meeting in Action

Like many classrooms, my class always had a buddy classroom. Fostering cross-age relationships can help build students' sense of relatedness and help them develop social skills such as compassion, empathy, and responsibility. Involving students in deciding what to do when meeting with a buddy classroom also provides a powerful opportunity for them to feel some control and to foster sound decision making. Here is a snapshot of one class meeting I held with older students to consider what to do with their second-grade buddies when they came for their first visit, to join us at our daily community gathering:

1. **Introduction:** I let the class know that all year, we would be paired with the second graders as buddies. Students had previous experience with buddy classrooms, so I did not need to elaborate much on what this meant. For our first visit, I explained, our second-grade buddies would join us for one of our daily class gatherings.

2. **Topic:** I shared with students the goal of the buddies program: to help students in our school feel more connected to each other, especially helping the younger students feel safer and more comfortable at school, and to help students develop skills like caring for other people and getting along with those of a different age. Then I shared a little about the more specific goals for this first meeting among buddies: to help our class get to know the younger students, to help the younger students feel comfortable when they came together, and to have some fun together.

   I asked students if they remembered what it was like to be in a younger class with older buddies. Several students shared some of their memories, helping all of them develop empathy by considering how nervous and anxious the younger students might feel.

3. *Suggestions:* Then I asked students to consider what activities we might do with the younger students in light of their possible nerves and so that they would want to return on future visits. Students' suggestions reflected their understanding of their buddies' needs. All the recommendations were for low-key activities that would be fun but not "over the top," as one student put it. For example:

→ making a book together, with each buddy pair contributing a page

→ completing a Venn diagram about what each pair of buddies had in common and how they differed

→ playing a ball-toss game

→ playing the Warm Wind Blows with pairs as teams[1]

→ having buddy pairs play a game just between them, such as a card game

→ reading a book together

→ giving options that each buddy pair could do together and letting the pairs choose

4. *Decision:* I began by asking the group to reflect on the list. "Look at the list. How did you do in meeting our goals for this first meeting with buddies?" This question gave students a chance to recognize their good work as a class—to see that their choices met the goals for this first get-together and showed care for their second graders. It also helped to reinforce importance of the goals as we moved into the decision phase of the meeting.

I then asked students to use a show of hands to indicate their top three activities. I went down the list and made tally marks as students raised their hands for various options. The top finalists

---

[1] In this game, the person who is it (in this case, a buddy pair) stands in the middle of the circle. The person's chair (in this case, chairs) is removed from the circle. The person (in this case, a buddy pair) identifies a category, such as people who like dogs. Those who fit in that category (in this case, a buddy pair) have to get up and find new seats with the person (in this case, the buddy pair) that cannot find a new seat, becoming the next it.

included playing a ball-toss game; playing the Warm Wind Blows in teams; and giving options that each buddy pair could do together and letting the pairs choose.

I invited students to speak on these options, and several spoke in favor of the one offering choice. One student suggested that tossing a ball might be harder for second graders than he initially thought, so he was beginning to doubt that one. I then asked students to use their thumbs to show which options they could live with, which they preferred, and which they thought we should drop. On that round, it became very clear that the class had moved toward a consensus on the third option, providing choice.

→ **Conclusion:** I pointed out the result, and students were excited. We quickly compiled a list of possible options using many suggestions from the initial list and adding one more, which was doing a drawing together. Given that the reaching-consensus stage is the hardest part of the meeting, I then gave students a few minutes to do a quickwrite about how that portion of the meeting went and what we could improve the next time we met. Also see Figure 6.2 for a planning sheet to use with students.

Class Meeting Planning Worksheet

1. *Introduction*
   - *For meetings at the beginning of the year*: What rules will you use to govern your class meetings? How will you invite students' input on these?

   - *For meetings later in the year*: Which rules will be particularly helpful for the topic of the meeting? How can you lead students to reflect on the importance of these rules and how they will look in action?

2. *Topic*
   - What are some topics or events for which you might seek class input?

   - How will you introduce the decision to be made or the event to be planned together?

   - What are the goals of the particular project or event that students should strive to address as they consider options and make a decision?

   - What will students have input on, and what aspects will be off the table?

   - How will you explore what students already know about this area or what their experience has been?

   - If students have no familiarity with the topic, how can you jump-start their thinking?

3. *Suggestions*
   - What structures will you use to foster all students' engagement?

4. *Decision*
   - How will you guide students to decide among the options?

5. *Conclusion*
   - What next steps do you anticipate students will need to take?

   - What rules or behaviors might you want to have students reflect on?

Figure 6.2

{ strategy }

Offer Choice

Another way to provide more autonomy is to offer students options whenever possible in social or academic settings or both. Choices can be as simple as where to do one's independent work—for example, sitting at a desk, standing, or sitting on the floor. Other choices might be more complex. For example, during a unit on insects, my students had an initial choice of which insect to study, and then after completing the same research steps, they had an additional choice of how to present what they learned. See Figure 6.3 for more ideas on how to offer choices to students.

Similarly, choices can be open, such as choosing any book to read for independent reading. Or students can choose from a list of teacher-created options. When providing a list, however, be careful not to overwhelm students with too many choices. Having too many options paralyzes many students, who, as a result, spend undue amounts of time trying to figure out what to do and then often have buyer's remorse and want to switch choices.

The following table offers ideas for providing choice in the classroom.

OPPORTUNITIES FOR CHOICE IN THE CLASSROOM	
	Choices
Social	• Inviting someone else to play at recess or sit with them at lunch (structured so that everyone is either an inviter or an invitee) • Choosing among several options for recess (sandbox, sidewalk activities, sports, laps, etc.) • Choosing among options during free times, such as indoor recess or visits from a buddy classroom • Deciding among certain options for how to commemorate or celebrate key events as a class • Choosing what work to display on a classroom display
Academic	Being able to choose the following (either openly or from a teacher-selected range of options): • What to read, write, or research • One of several options that are all designed to meet the same learning goal—for example, for students learning math facts, the options might be flash cards, online quiz games, and worksheets • Completing a worksheet or correcting a completed worksheet that has errors that need to be identified and fixed • A more challenging option • How to demonstrate learning at the end of a lesson or unit • Whether to write in pencil or pen • Whether to stand or sit during a task • Where to work

Figure 6.3

Students need to be set up for success with choices. Spell out your expectations (Will students be able to change their minds once they start?) and make sure students understand what each choice entails. For example, when giving students a choice of where to work, it helps to tie that choice to an expectation that they be productive and to discuss what that means. If you give students a choice of two different academic options, you must first thoroughly teach how to do each task for the choice to be meaningful and worthwhile.

It also helps for students frequently to reflect on how they did with choices. Doing so helps them develop skills with decision making and evaluation and learn that exercising one's autonomy comes with certain responsibilities. For example, after students have had a choice, you might ask, "Would you make the same choice again? Why or why not?" and "Did your choice help you learn or practice the target skill?" See Figure 6.4 to plan for using choice effectively.

{commitment}

Identify and Expand on
Social and Academic Choices

What choices do you currently offer in your classroom?

Social	Academic

What are two additional ways you could add choice?

Social	Academic

How are you teaching or how could you teach students how to be responsible with regard to the choices they make? _____

How can you help students reflect on their choices, connecting choice with consequence? _____

_____

Figure 6.4

{ strategy }

Foster Autonomy
Through Curriculum

Engaging students in meaningful work at your school or in the community can also increase their sense of autonomy. For instance, one of the teachers at a school where I worked challenged his eighth graders to undertake a change project. They had to look for an area or habit in the school that was problematic, research the background that led to it, analyze or explain why it was problematic, and propose a realistic and doable change. Students were quite invested in this project, and the fact that they had both choice and control throughout the project allowed them to feel ownership and success.

Be on the lookout for ways to infuse the curriculum with texts, problems, and discussions that will particularly resonate with students. For example:

→ Have students research local issues or projects in connection with social studies, science, or math.

→ Occasionally choose books that students bring to your attention or that touch on events of particular interest or connection to the lives of your students to use as texts for English language arts or read-alouds.

→ Provide opportunities for students to participate in meaningful science investigations or data collection, such as the many citizen science projects available online.

→ When teaching units or topics with which students do not have much experience or knowledge, take the time to help them build needed background knowledge and understand why the topic matters.

{ shift }

Collaborate with Students

Often, especially for children who struggle, we step in to try to dictate how they can and should solve various challenges they face. For a student who frequently gets upset, we might say, "I want you to count to ten every time you feel upset." For a child who struggles with getting along with classmates, we might require that the child find three nice things to say about his partner during an activity. Our efforts are well meaning but sometimes fail, leaving us and the child frustrated.

They might fail for several reasons. Children often are not sufficiently invested in strategies we choose. Also they sometimes may not sufficiently understand why we're asking them to use a given strategy or how it's connected to anything. The strategy we choose might not even address the reason the child is experiencing the underlying problem. Perhaps most importantly, when we impose solutions, we undercut children's sense of autonomy, and for many of our most troubled students, this simply adds insult to injury.

A solution to these issues is to involve children in solving their own problems. Sometimes you can do this informally. For example, if a child has made a mess, you can simply show her where cleaning materials are or ask, "Do you need help figuring out how to clean this up?" These informal conversations might also involve giving a child a choice. For example, if a child is struggling to organize his thoughts for writing, a teacher might ask, "Do you want to dictate some notes to me, or would you rather use sentence frames?"

At other times, however, we might want to engage in more structured conversations to address problems with students. The benefits of these structured conversations often stretch well beyond the problem the child and you have set out to work on. They can help you and the child break prior negative patterns of interacting, focusing both of you on new possibilities and strategies for success. They can help students feel more connected, autonomous, and hopeful, and the ripple effects of these feelings can in turn make the child more socially acceptable and academically successful. A small investment of time can have big payoffs.

{ strategy }

Use a Protocol for Teacher-Student Conversations

As with the protocol for teachers we described in Section 3, there are many variations for how to structure formal conversations between teachers and students. It can be helpful to keep the protocol simple enough to be used flexibly across situations. The teacher-student conversation protocol adapted from Crowe (2009) is simple and flexible:

1. Introduction

2. Problem

3. Underlying causes

4. Suggestions

5. Closing

Here is a brief overview of what each step entails:

1. **Introduction:** To begin the conversation, it is helpful to make some meaningful personal connection with the student. Just as our adult meetings are often more productive if we begin with a little time to connect personally, children often relax and are more mentally prepared to take on challenges if they have a few minutes to talk with us personally. For example, you might find out how some event in the child's life (sports game, concert, test in another subject, etc.) went, share news about some common interest ("Did you hear that the Patriots signed a new defensive back yesterday?"), or remind the child of a shared happy moment ("Are you enjoying reading *Love That Dog*? I can't wait to read more today to see what happens.").

   Then briefly explain why you wanted to meet, being as direct as possible. "I am glad we have some time to talk today. I wanted to discuss a problem [challenge] I've been noticing and see what we can figure out."

2. **Problem:** Identify the problem from your viewpoint, using facts, not generalizations or labels. This is very similar to the presentation of the problem to colleagues in the protocol shared in Section 3. Simply describe what you've seen and why it matters. Then invite the child's input by using open-ended questions and listen to what he has to say. You might just ask, "What have you noticed about this problem?" Or you might ask, "What has been happening from your point of view?" I have learned so much from actively listening to children's answers. Often I find something out that I didn't know before. There have been several times when I just stopped the conversation at this point because I wanted to think more and gather more evidence about what the child said, particularly if the child noticed vastly different things from what I had experienced.

   When the child's observations are close to yours, which often happens, use some language that invites or encourages the child to work on addressing the problem with you.

   Avoid using the word *solving* with children. This helps both them and us keep our expectations for these challenges realistic. Many challenges all of us face are ongoing and can't necessarily be solved, especially in a brief conversation. A child who struggles to make connections with friends may need many conversations (as well as other strategies) over the course of the years to make progress.

   Instead, say something like, "Would you like to work on this problem together?" or "Would you like to think about this challenge a bit more with me?" If the child agrees, keep going with the next step in the protocol.

   Very infrequently, a child might say that he doesn't want to work on the problem. You should, of course, honor this, as one key aspect of the conversation is to build the child's sense of autonomy. However, if the child seems comfortable, pursue what his reasoning for not wanting to proceed is. His reasons could be very illuminating.

3. **Causes:** During this step, you and the child will delve more deeply into what is going on. You might ask, "Why do you think this happens [or keeps happening]?" Again, sometimes I was amazed by

what children had to say here. I have found out children's parents were getting divorced, they were being bullied, or, in one case, the child simply had a complete misunderstanding of what another teacher expected in his class.

However, often, students have no idea what's going on. When asked, they give the shrug teachers universally recognize as "I dunno." Because of this very real possibility, you should come prepared to provide some ideas of what might be going on but do so with humility and without commitment to any one cause. For example, you might say, "Well, of course, I don't know either, but I'm wondering about some of these possibilities. Maybe . . ." Then see what the child thinks about the possibilities you raised. You might not be able to pinpoint an exact cause, and that is OK. Even if you and the child just begin to get some sense of what is going on, that could be a meaningful step forward.

4. **Suggestions:** Discuss with the child ideas for how to ameliorate the problem. Begin by asking if the child has any ideas. Doing so will validate her feelings of competence and autonomy. Sometimes children have remarkable ideas about what might help them. Try to be open to working with some of their suggestions, even if they will take some massaging to become practical.

   If the child doesn't have any idea, be prepared to offer a few of your own. Discuss these with the child and get her input. Sometimes it may seem that nothing either of you has come up with so far will help ameliorate the problem. Again, try to remember that the goal is to make progress, not to find quick fixes. In this instance, it may help to stop and each do more thinking.

   At other times, a suggestion or two will really resonate with a child, and she might want to go forward with them. Again, this is a conversation, not an assignment, so let the child take the lead in choosing what to do next.

5. **Closing:** How you close the meeting really depends upon what happens in the prior step. If you and the student spent a lot of time brainstorming, you might just agree to keep thinking about the issue and make a plan for another meeting. Or, if the student found

a strategy that he really liked, you might agree to try it out and then discuss how long that trial period will be, how you will know if it is working, and when you might touch base again.

Teacher-Student Conversation Protocol in Action: Example 1

Here's an example of how the protocol can look in action, based on my work with Alanna. I had tried being proactive by reminding her of the expectations before work times and using firm redirecting language and reasonable and related consequences for her behaviors but with only temporary and mildly successful results. Knowing that these collaborations were most successful when narrow, I decided to begin with only one tiny aspect of the problem: her following me around the room to talk when she was supposed to be engaged in academic work.

1. *Introduction:* Alanna was happy to have me to herself and began the personal connection part of the meeting. She had an interest in fashion and began by offering me tips on my outfit. We laughed a little about how I would never be able to teach in the kind of shoes she wished I would wear. Then I was able to take the reins and segue into our topic. "You and I always have such great conversations, and I enjoy talking to you. Today, though, I want to talk about something I've noticed: the timing of our conversations."

2. *Problem:* I had written out in advance and practiced what I would say at this point, as I wanted it to be factual and not something that would make her question our relationship. "Here's a problem I've been noticing: I've noticed that often when it is time for you to be working at your desk, you get up to tell me something. Yesterday I kept a tally and noticed that you were out of your seat seventeen times. I've noticed that you have a hard time concentrating on your work and finishing it as a result." I had a lot more data and concerns but didn't want to overwhelm her.

    At this point I invited Alanna to reflect: "What have you seen happening at independent work times?"

    She was pretty open. "I've noticed the same thing. I have a lot I want to say to you."

To make sure she agreed that her tendency to follow me around and talk to me was actually a problem, I followed up by asking, "What have you noticed about getting your work done?" She agreed that she was often not completing tasks. So I asked, "Would you like to work on this together?" She agreed, so we moved on to the next step.

3. **Causes:** I explained that often to work on a problem successfully, we have to understand why it's happening. I asked her if she had some ideas about why she found it hard to stay focused on her work and wanted to talk to me instead. She reiterated how much she liked talking to me. I let her know that I enjoyed our conversations too, but I also wanted her to have time for learning and to make sure I could do my job of supporting her and her classmates during these times.

    I also had a suspicion that although she was surviving with her academic work, she might have some fear or challenges with it. Accordingly, I asked, "I'm wondering if in addition to enjoying our conversations, there's something about the work you're having trouble with." She told me that she was actually feeling a little unsure of both math and writing. This was great information for me to have and led to ideas for some other support I was able to offer her in the future.

4. **Suggestions:** I then told her we should spend some time thinking about ways to improve the situation and asked if she had any ideas. She did not really, so I suggested a few options I had prepared in advance:

    → *Tokens:* I would give her a certain amount of talking tokens for the day and once they were used up, she had to stay in her seat.

    → A *topic notebook*: I already kept conversation journals with my students in which we wrote back and forth daily, but I suggested she might enjoy keeping a separate notebook with a running list of topics to discuss with me that we could use to chat at free times. She could keep it at her desk and, instead of getting up, just write one word to help her remember her topic.

- ➤ *A timer:* I let her know that some students benefited from working for a set amount of time before taking a break using a timer.

- ➤ *Help with structuring work time:* I also offered the idea of helping her divide up work so as not to feel too overwhelmed.

  She immediately latched onto the first option and was quite excited about trying it.

5. **Closing:** We talked about how many tokens we should start with. Given that her average was about fifteen interruptions a day, I suggested we start with five tokens for the day. I figured we could always work our way down. She agreed, and we decided to check back in another week to see how things were going.

To be honest, I did not have much confidence in the token solution. It wouldn't have been my first choice. But, to my surprise, the tokens actually worked. Somehow having the autonomy to help select a strategy worked in a way that my reminders and consequences had not. At our check-in meeting the next week, we decided to cut the tokens down by one a week. During that time period I also worked to develop some other scaffolds for writing and math, which undoubtedly helped as well. By the middle of the year she was able to successfully work independently. We did have other problems to work on, but the use of the protocol gave us some success from which to move forward.

Teacher-Student Conversation Protocol in Action: Example 2

As I stated at the outset, the protocol needs to be used flexibly. What follows is based on a conversation a teacher I coached had with a child who struggled to connect with peers for a number of reasons. The teacher decided to focus on one reason with which she thought the child should encounter some success—the child's failure to follow socially acceptable norms for eating lunch. In the conversation that resulted, the teacher decided to skip the "Causes" step because it was immaterial to the conference. Also, the student wanted time to think about the options the teacher described, so the conference did not lead to any immediate strategies but merely to another conference.

1. **Introduction:** The teacher knew the student loved Star Wars movies and building sets. She began by asking the child what he had been working on lately. He happily shared some of his recent building success. When a natural pause occurred, the teacher said, "I would love to see a picture of what you made. Feel free to bring it in. I wanted to talk with you today about lunch and how I can help make that a happier time for you."

2. **Problem:** Noticing that the child seemed to brighten at that possibility, the teacher said, "Remember last week how you told me that Justin had hurt your feelings by saying he didn't want to sit with you?" The child nodded. The teacher then reminded the student that she had come to lunch twice since then to observe what was happening. She then went on, "I expect everyone in our class to be kind to you and will always help ensure that happens. But when I was at lunch, I also observed some things that you might not even know you're doing that might make it harder for people to want to be with you at lunch. Would you like to hear more about that?" The child said he would, so the teacher continued by saying, "I noticed that often when you eat, you put a big bite or several bites in your mouth at once. That makes it hard to close your mouth so people see the inside. I also noticed that sometimes you get so excited about a topic that you talk when you are eating, so some of that food falls out." The teacher then asked, "What have you noticed or heard from others about your eating?" The child said that his parents had often talked to him about the way he ate, but it was just the way he was, and he wasn't sure he could help it. The teacher asked if he was interested in trying, and the child agreed.

3. **Causes:** The teacher had decided before the conference that it didn't really matter why the child had developed poor table manners. She chose to skip this step.

4. **Suggestions:** The teacher asked the child if he had any ideas of how to get better. She wasn't surprised based on his earlier answers that he shrugged and shook his head. With a colleague's help, she had prepared a few ideas in advance:

→ *Reading about table manners*: The teacher knew the child enjoyed reading and had found an interesting book about table manners in different countries. She suggested the child might enjoy reading it first.

→ *Practicing with the teacher*: The teacher offered to have a private lunch with the child several times in a row and coach the child with eating.

→ *Working with the family*: Another strategy was for the teacher to work with the child's family to come up with some practice ideas for home.

→ *Watching videos*: The teacher had found numerous videos online in which people taught table manners.

The child asked the teacher to write the strategies down for him. He wasn't sure what to do but wanted to think about it.

5. **Closing:** The teacher concluded by saying, "You were very brave to listen to me talk about this problem. I know it wasn't that easy. You can let me know what you decide."

A few days later, the child said he was ready to meet again. During that conversation, he first suggested that he try all the solutions, but the teacher was worried about that being overwhelming, so she asked him to choose his top two. Figure 6.5 is a helpful tool for this planning. He began the process by choosing the book and the videos.

Teacher-Student Conversation Protocol Planning Sheet

The more strategically you plan for these conversations, the more likely they will be effective in helping the child improve and feel more competent and autonomous.
Use this worksheet to guide your preparation.

Focusing the Conversation

What is the issue you want to discuss with the child?

_____

_____

_____

What factual information do you have about this issue?

_____

_____

_____

If you do not have much factual information, when, where, and how will you collect it?

_____

_____

_____

Planning What to Say

Introduction: How will you personally connect with the child?

_____

_____

_____

continues

Teacher-Student Conversation Protocol
Planning Sheet, *continued*

Problem: How will you neutrally describe the problem to the child?

_____

_____

_____

Causes: What are some possible reasons for the problem?

_____

_____

_____

Suggestions: What are some strategies you might suggest to the child?

_____

_____

_____

Closing: Decide how the student will proceed and when you will follow up to talk about how well it's going.

_____

_____

_____

Figure 6.5

Reflection

Facilitating these conversations is a skill that takes time and strategic practice to develop. To be strategic, it helps to formally or informally reflect on how the conversation went and in particular what we did well in our facilitation and might need to do better the next time.

Essentials for Success

Keep the following tips in mind as you plan for the conference to help ensure its success.

➤ *Make sure the challenge is appropriate for a child's collaboration.* Not all problems are suitable for this conversation protocol. For example, a child who suffers from extreme anxiety most likely needs professional intervention first. The child and you might then try some strategies suggested in this setting and confer about how those are working. But it is unrealistic to think the child can address such overwhelming problems on her own.

➤ *Make sure this isn't your first private conversation with the child.* Imagine you had a colleague, boss, or friend who talked to you only when he wanted to address a problem. You wouldn't ever want to talk to him! Before scheduling the conversation with a student, be sure that she and you have had plenty of other opportunities for private chats, even if those were brief. Also make sure that they continue after the formal protocol conversation occurs.

➤ *Be sure you have a sufficiently strong relationship with the child.* These conferences can bolster our relationships with students and increase their own sense of relatedness, competence, and autonomy, but they just will not work without at least some initial relationship between you and the student. The child has to have a strong enough relationship with you to be able to trust you to talk, explore possibilities, and embrace the unknown that problem solving can offer. If you still have a long way to go in getting to know a student, hold off on having a conference.

→ *Choose the problem carefully.* Often the children with whom we want to have these conferences have many issues that we need to address. Resist the temptation to try to tackle all of those at once. I always remind myself it would be like asking me to work on weight loss, give up Diet Coke, and improve my household organization all at the same time. Choose a problem with which a child can encounter some success. For example, consider problems that will be fairly simple to address even if they are not the most pressing ones, as success in one area will breed your and the student's confidence to take on another challenge. Or choose the most pressing problem—the one that is especially getting in the way of the student's work, her relationships with peers, or her relationship with you—but set your and the child's expectations for the results from the first conversation fairly low.

→ *Prepare with a trusted colleague.* By the time you get to the point of wanting to have a private conference, you're likely to have tried quite a few strategies with a child. You might even be feeling frustrated. Seek out a colleague to help you plan for the conference using the previous guide. That colleague can help you think more divergently about what's going on, so that you can present the problem factually, propose meaningful possible causes for the problem, and suggest reasonable interventions.

→ *Be open to the child's input.* Listen and be open to what the child has to say. Students can surprise us with their insights, reveal new information, or come up with interventions we never would have thought of. It is critical not to come to the conversation with preconceived notions of what should happen at each step.

→ *Keep the meetings private.* This can be challenging in small classrooms loaded with children. Consider having a private lunch meeting or a meeting before or after school. If really pressed, I sometimes prevailed upon a trusted colleague or administrator to take my class for a read-aloud or just to supervise independent reading time while I met with a child. You might have to get creative to find time and privacy, but the results will be worth it.

Looking Inward and Outward

> *Every thought you produce, anything you say, any action you do, it bears your signature.*
> —**Thich Nhat Hanh,** *Peace Is Every Step: The Path of Mindfulness in Everyday Life*

It is a rare individual who has a purpose, a moral compass so clear, that he or she is able to act consistently with courage almost instinctively, regardless of comfort or risk. They are the ones who leap to the front of our minds—MLK, Gandhi, Rosa, Malala. We know *them* well; they are our heroes.

Perhaps though, their heroism is a problem for *us*. As a society, we've canonized their activism as something outside of normal human behavior instead of understanding it as part of it, part of who each of us is. To ponder their sacrifices as our own can feel too heavy an expectation; it's too much to ask that we be better than we are in this moment. But maybe the mistake we make is when we think we have to be them to do the work that needs doing, to be the story we tell ourselves about them, as if heroism involves surrendering one's entire self to an idea with absolute purity. That's a story that contradicts the reality of being human and prevents us from taking simple actions that can improve the lives of our students. Each of us has the capacity to disrupt patterns of behavior that aren't supportive of our classroom communities. Maybe not in every second of every day, but in enough moments to matter. As we hope we've shown through our own experiences with students, we can examine and own our stresses, our preferences, our expectations of cultural and behavioral norms, and the biases we bring to the classroom. We can operate with the belief that children, no matter who they are, where they come from, or what they look like, can and do learn, and that their learning only gets better as their teachers become better.

In her 2015 commencement address at Martin Luther King Jr. Early College Prep, Michelle Obama cites her mother's response to praise of her son Craig and daughter

Michelle as exceptional and unusually talented. "They're not special at all. The South Side is filled with kids like that" (Obama 2015). What made the difference for her children, what can make the difference for any child regardless of circumstances, is that Craig and Michelle knew they were cared for, that someone had faith in their full potential and would help them be their best selves. And Michelle Obama, in her recent memoir *Becoming*, describes how she carries that idea forward, interacting with as many young people as possible to let them know that "all of [them] belong here" (2018, 367) in a community that values achievement and recognizes theirs. Rita Pierson, in the well known 2013 Ted Talk of the same title said, "Every child needs a champion." You can become that for the children in your classroom.

We can look *inward* to examine what biases or fears keep us from caring enough about the children in our classroom. With that greater understanding, we can then look *outward* to see the children in front of us clearly, the children who are much more than whatever behavior we see in that moment that is giving us pause. We don't have to be heroes to do the work our classroom communities require of us. The kids we can't reach today can become the kids we reach tomorrow.

The reality is that most of us are faced with difficult decisions about how to interact with our students multiple times every day, and we have to make on-the-spot decisions every time. We'll never be perfect, but I have seen enough teachers become so much better, more successful, and more caring than they were, that I believe we all can be better if we commit to trying.

Will you accept an invitation to try something this book has suggested? Sometimes the greatest change and awakening comes for us when it is an invitation to embark on a journey of personal discovery, an invitation to try, an invitation to look inward for reflection and outward for connection. You might not expect it to go well, but you also might be surprised at how good it feels. It might change what you think you believe. It might even change your life. It might even change the lives of the children you teach.

Accept the invitation. Not just for the children who conform to expectations but for the ones who don't, those who feel hardest to connect with. The child who looks nothing like us, the one who interrupts, calls out, struggles, doesn't finish homework or classwork, the one who gets into fights and who talks right back at us . . . that's the child who needs to be in the forefront of our minds. That child has to be the one we are committed to teaching, the one whom we make feel safe and cared for, the one whom we help feel relatedness, competence, and autonomy.

How will you show your students you care? What signature will you leave on your classroom community?

Works Cited

Anderson, Mike. 2010. *The Well-Balanced Teacher: How to Work Smarter and Stay Sane Inside the Classroom and Out*. Alexandria, VA: Association for Supervision and Curriculum Development.

Aud, Susan, William Hussar, Frank Johnson, Grace Kena, Erin Roth, Eileen Manning, Xiaolei Wang, and Jijun Zhang. 2012. *The Condition of Education 2012*. Washington, DC: National Center for Education Statistics, US Department of Education.

Birch, Sondra H., and Gary W. Ladd. 1997. "The Teacher-Child Relationship and Children's Early School Adjustment." *Journal of School Psychology* 35 (1): 61–79.

Blum, Robert W., and Heather P. Libbey. 2004. "School Connectedness: Strengthening the Health and Education Outcomes for Teenagers." *Journal of School Health* 74 (4): 229–99.

Cambourne, Brian. 2002. "Conditions for Literacy Learning: The Conditions of Learning: Is Learning Natural?" *The Reading Teacher* 55 (8): 758–62.

Cassetta, Gianna, and Brook Sawyer. 2013. *No More Taking Away Recess and Other Problematic Discipline Practices*. Portsmouth, NH: Heinemann.

———.2015. *Classroom Management Matters: The Social-Emotional Learning Approach Children Deserve*. Portsmouth, NH: Heinemann.

Charney, Ruth Sidney. 2015. *Teaching Children to Care: Classroom Management for Ethical and Academic Growth, K–8*. Turner Falls, MA: Center for Responsive Schools, Inc.

Cohen, Randy. 2009. "Nesting Blues." *The New York Times Magazine*, July 15. www.nytimes.com/2009/07/19/magazine/19FOB-ethicist-t.html.

Coolahan, Kathleen, John Fantuzzo, Julia Mendez, and Paul McDermott. 2000. "Preschool Peer Interactions and Readiness to Learn: Relationships Between Classroom Peer Play and Learning Behaviors and Conduct." *Journal of Educational Psychology* 92: 458–65.

Crowe, Caltha. 2009. *Solving Thorny Behavior Problems: How Teachers and Students Can Work Together*. Turner Falls, MA: Center for Responsive Schools, Inc.

Deci, Edward L. and Richard M. Ryan. 1985. *Intrinsic Motivation and Self-Determination in Human Behavior*. New York: Plenum Press.

DeMonte, Jenny, and Robert Hanna. 2014. "Looking at the Best Teachers and Who They Teach: Poor Students and Students of Color Are Less Likely to Get Highly Effective Teaching." Center of American Progress. www .americanprogress.org/issues/education-k-12/reports/2014/04/11/87683 /looking-at-the-best-teachers-and-who-they-teach/.

Denton, Paula. 2015. *The Power of Our Words: Teacher Language That Helps Children Learn*. Turner Falls, MA: Center for Responsive Schools.

DePaoli, Jennifer L., Matthew N. Atwell, and John Bridgeland. 2017. *Ready to Lead: A National Principal Survey on How Social and Emotional Learning Can Prepare Children and Transform Schools*. A Report for CASEL. Washington, DC: Civic Enterprises.

Dweck, Carol S. 2007. *Mindset: The New Psychology of Success*. New York: Ballantine Books.

Finn, Jeremy D., Gina Pannozzo, Charles M. Achilles. 2003. "The 'Why's' of Class Size: Student Behavior in Small Classes." Research Article https://doi.org/10.3102/00346543073003321.

Ginott, Haim G. 1972. *Teacher and Child: A Book for Parents and Teachers*. New York: Macmillan.

Giovanni, Nikki. 1970. *Black Feelings, Black Talk, Black Judgement*. New York: William Morrow.

Goleman, Daniel. 1995. *Emotional Intelligence: Why It Can Matter More Than IQ*. New York: Bantam Books.

———. 2015. *A Force for Good: The Dalai Lama's Vision for Our World*. New York: Bantam Books.

Graziano, Paulo A., Rachael D. Reavis, Susan P. Keane, and Susan D. Calkins. 2007. "The Role of Emotion Regulation in Children's Early Academic Success." *Journal of School Psychology* 45 (1): 3–19.

Greenberg, Mark T., Roger P. Weissberg, Mary U. O'Brien, Joseph E. Zins, Linda Fredericks, Hank Resnik, and Maurice J. Elias. 2003. "Enhancing School-Based Prevention and Youth Development Through Coordinated Social, Emotional, and Academic Learning." *American Psychologist* 58 (6–7): 466–74.

Hanh, Thich Nhat, and Katherine Weare. 2017. *Happy Teachers Change the World: A Guide for Cultivating Mindfulness in Education*. Berkeley, CA: Parallax.

Hoy, Anita W., and Carol S. Weinstein. 2006. "Student and Teacher Perspectives on Classroom Management." In *Handbook of Classroom Management: Research, Practice, and Contemporary Issues*, ed. Carolyn M. Evertson and Carol S. Weinstein, 181–219. New York: Routledge.

Hughes, J. N., W. Lou, O. M. Kwok, and L. K. Loyd. 2008. "Teacher–Student Support, Effortful Engagement, and Achievement: A 3-Year Longitudinal Study." *Journal of Educational Psychology* 100: 1–14. doi:10.1037/0022-0663.100.1.1.

Javernick, Ellen. 2010. *What If Everybody Did That?* Tarrytown, NY: Pinwheel Books.

Johnston, Peter H. 2004. *Choice Words: How Our Language Affects Children's Learning.* Portland, ME: Stenhouse.

———. 2012. *Opening Minds: Using Language to Change Lives.* Portland, ME: Stenhouse.

Joy, Melanie. 2008. *Why We Love Dogs, Eat Pigs, and Wear Cows: An Introduction to Carnism.* Newburyport, MA: Red Wheel/Weiser.

Kain, Philip J. 1943. *Hegel and the Other: A Study of the Phenomenology of Spirit.* SUNY series in Hegelian studies. Albany, NY: SUNY Press.

Klem, Adena M. and James Patrick Connell. 2004. "Relationships Matter: Linking Teacher Support to Student Engagement and Achievement." *Journal of School Health* 74. 262–73.

Lally, Phillippa, Cornelia H. M. van Jaarsveld, Henry W. W. Potts, and Jane Wardle. 2009. "How Are Habits Formed? Modelling Habit Formation in the Real World." *European Journal of Social Psychology* 40 (6): 998–1009. https://onlinelibrary.wiley.com/doi/abs/10.1002/ejsp.674.

Mullainathan, Sendhil. 2015. "Police Killings of Blacks: Here Is What the Data Say." *The New York Times*, Oct. 16. www.nytimes.com/2015/10/18/upshot/police-killings-of-blacks-what-the-data-says.html.

Normandeau, S., and F. Guay. 1998. "Preschool Behavior and First-Grade School Achievement: The Meditational Role of Cognitive Self-Control." *Journal of Educational Psychology* 90: 111–21.

Obama, Michelle. 2015. Chicago Tribune, June 9 Transcript of Michelle Obama's Commencement Address ((https://www.chicagotribune.com/news/ct-michelle-obama-commencement-address-transcript-20150609-story.html)

———. 2018. *Becoming.* New York: Crown.

Oxford Reference. https://www.oxfordreference.com/view/10./1093/oi/authority.20110803100005347Palacio, R. J. 2012. *Wonder.* New York: Random House.

Palacio, R. J. 2012. *Wonder.* New York: Random House.

Patrick, Helen, Julianne C. Turner, Debra K. Meyer, and Carol Midgley. 2003. "How Teachers Establish Psychological Environments During the First Days of School: Associations with Avoidance in Mathematics." *Teachers College Record* 105: 1521–58. doi:10.1111/1467-9620.00299.

Pianta, Robert C. 1999. *Enhancing Relationships Between Children and Teachers.* Washington, DC: American Psychological Association.

Pierson, Rita. 2013. "Every Child Needs a Champion." Filmed
    April 2013 in New York. TED video, 7:21. www.ted.com/talks/
    rita_pierson_every_kid_needs_a_champion?language=en#t-11407.

Quaglia Institute for Student Aspirations. 2008. *My Voice Student Report 2008*. Port-
    land, ME: Quaglia Institute for Student Aspirations. http://quagliainstitute
    .org/dmsView/MyVoice6-12StudentNationalReport-Analysis2008.

Responsive Classroom. 2015. *The First Six Weeks of School*. 2nd ed. Turners Falls,
    MA: Center for Responsive Schools.

Roorda, Debora L., Helma M. Y. Koomen, Jantine L. Spilt, and Frans J. Oort. 2011.
    "The Influence of Affective Teacher–Student Relationships on Students'
    School Engagement and Achievement." *Review of Educational Research* 81 (4):
    493–529. doi:10.3102/0034654311421793.

Rose, Todd. 2016. "How the Idea of a 'Normal' Person Got Invented." *The Atlantic*,
    Feb. 18. www.theatlantic.com/business/archive/2016/02/the-invention-of
    -the-normal-person/463365/.

Senge, Peter. 1990. *The 5th Discipline*. New York: Doubleday.

U.S. Department of Education. 2016. Civil Rights Data Collection. https://ocrdata
    .ed.gov/.

Watson, Marilyn, and Victor Battistich. 2006. "Building and Sustaining Caring
    Communities." In *Handbook of Classroom Management: Research, Practice,
    and Contemporary Issues*, ed. Carolyn M. Evertson and Carol S. Weinstein,
    253–80. New York: Routledge.

Wentzel, K. R. 1993. "Does being good make the grade? Social behavior and
    academic competence in middle school." *Journal of Educational Psychology*
    90 (2): 202–09.

Wood, Chip, and Babs Freeman-Loftis. 2011. *Responsive School Discipline: Essen-
    tials for Elementary School Leaders*. Turner Falls, MA: Center for Responsive
    Schools, Inc.